# 1,000,000 Books

are available to read at

www.ForgottenBooks.com

Read online
Download PDF
Purchase in print

ISBN 978-1-332-04645-4
PIBN 10275394

This book is a reproduction of an important historical work. Forgotten Books uses
state-of-the-art technology to digitally reconstruct the work, preserving the original format
whilst repairing imperfections present in the aged copy. In rare cases, an imperfection in
the original, such as a blemish or missing page, may be replicated in our edition. We do,
however, repair the vast majority of imperfections successfully; any imperfections that
remain are intentionally left to preserve the state of such historical works.

Forgotten Books is a registered trademark of FB &c Ltd.
Copyright © 2018 FB &c Ltd.
FB &c Ltd, Dalton House, 60 Windsor Avenue, London, SW19 2RR.
Company number 08720141. Registered in England and Wales.

For support please visit www.forgottenbooks.com

# 1 MONTH OF FREE READING

## at
## www.ForgottenBooks.com

By purchasing this book you are eligible for one month membership to ForgottenBooks.com, giving you unlimited access to our entire collection of over 1,000,000 titles via our web site and mobile apps.

To claim your free month visit: www.forgottenbooks.com/free275394

\* Offer is valid for 45 days from date of purchase. Terms and conditions apply.

English
Français
Deutsche
Italiano
Español
Português

www.forgottenbooks.com

**Mythology** Photography **Fiction**
Fishing Christianity **Art** Cooking
Essays Buddhism Freemasonry
Medicine **Biology** Music **Ancient Egypt** Evolution Carpentry Physics
Dance Geology **Mathematics** Fitness
Shakespeare **Folklore** Yoga Marketing
**Confidence** Immortality Biographies
Poetry **Psychology** Witchcraft
Electronics Chemistry History **Law**
Accounting **Philosophy** Anthropology
Alchemy Drama Quantum Mechanics
Atheism Sexual Health **Ancient History**
**Entrepreneurship** Languages Sport
Paleontology Needlework Islam
**Metaphysics** Investment Archaeology
Parenting Statistics Criminology
**Motivational**

# A COMPLETE SYSTEM

OF

# LATIN PROSODY;

FOR THE USE OF

SCHOOLS, COLLEGES, AND PRIVATE LEARNERS;

ON A PLAN ENTIRELY NEW:

BY PATRICK S. CASSERLY,

Formerly Principal of the Chrestomathic Institution, and Author of "A Translation of Jacobs' Greek Reader;" of "A New Literal Translation of Longinus on the Sublime;" of "The Little Garden of Roses, and Valley of Lilies," from the original Latin of Thomas à Kempis, &c., &c.

SECOND EDITION, REVISED AND IMPROVED.

Scandere qui nescis, versiculos laceras.—*Claudian.*

NEW YORK:
WILLIAM E. DEAN, No. 2 ANN STREET.

1847.

ENTERED, according to Act of Congress, in the year 1847,
BY WILLIAM E. DEAN,
In the Clerk's Office of the District Court of the United States for the Southern District of New York.

STEREOTYPED BY THOMAS B. SMITH
216 WILLIAM STREET, NEW YORK

TO

THE REV. JAMES R. BAYLEY, A.M.,

VICE PRESIDENT OF ST. JOHN'S COLLEGE, NEW YORK,

THIS LITTLE WORK,

INTENDED TO FACILITATE AN ACQUAINTANCE WITH

THE BEAUTIES OF THE LATIN LANGUAGE,

IS DEDICATED,

AS A TOKEN OF ESTEEM,

BY THE AUTHOR.

450401

# PREFACE.

AMONG the most highly polished nations, whether of ancient or of modern times, a knowledge of Latin Prosody has ever been regarded as a qualification, indispensable to every one claiming the reputation of a classical scholar. And, considering the intimate connexion subsisting between the knowledge of a learned language, —particularly of one so marvellously metrical as the Latin,—and that of its Prosody, this cannot seem strange: because without the latter, the former is, in some degree, unattainable, or at least imperfect.

With the single exception of the Greek, probably no language in the world can boast a versification, approximating that of the stately Roman. In beauty, sweetness, and melody, it is unrivalled: —in the admirable arrangement of its vowels and consonants, it is the perfection of art:—while the harmonious and ever varying recurrence of long and short syllables (in strict accordance with the nicest principles of music), has rendered Latin verse, for more than two thousand years, the purest standard of rhythmical and poetic excellence. To the most casual observer, then, it must be evident, that a knowledge of the Prosody regulating the accentuation as well as the pronunciation of this rich, majestic, and mellifluous tongue, is, with the classical scholar, not merely a matter of choice but of necessity.

No one certainly can pretend to *fully* understand a language which he cannot correctly read: but no one can read the sonorous and musical language of ancient Rome, without a thorough acquaintance with its Prosody; it thence follows that a knowledge of the latter is indispensable to a proper understanding of the former: yet how many are found among those calling themselves classical scholars, who can scarcely read a page in Virgil or Horace, much less of Homer, without perpetrating as many Prosodial blunders as there are lines—yea words—in the page! Why is this? Why of all countries in the world, should the United States, with the reputation of possessing the greatest number of colleges in proportion to the population, suffer the imputation of producing the worst Prosodians? Because in the United States, of all countries of the world, the Prosody of the learned languages has not received the attention which its importance demanded, or the more finished classical studies of other countries required of either professors or students. Another cause consequent on this—the general incompetence of teachers to impart a proper knowledge of its rules or their application, has probably proved more injurious to this branch of classical literature, than any other;—in numberless instances amounting to its partial neglect or even total desuetude: for men too often affect to despise or undervalue what they cannot appreciate or do not understand. From these and various other causes,* not forgetting that too operative, utilitarian, *cui bono* principle, which bears so powerful a sway over all studies and pursuits on this side of the Atlantic, the cultivation of this elegant acquirement has never received a due share of encouragement in the United States.

With the exception of two treatises by Professor Anthon, there has been no work deserving of the name, published in this country. One of these, however, was little more than a republication of the well known work written in Latin by the learned Jesuit Alvarez; with a translation of the rules and some few trifling corrections, and improvements: the other recently published, if not a more useful is a far more elaborate production; every way creditable to Professor Anthon's high reputation as a profound scholar and an accomplished Prosodian.

But to the compiler as well as to many other classical teachers, this latter, although a work of great merit and laborious research, has always appeared defective in two great essentials; viz., *comprehensive brevity* and *educational permanency*, both in its details and mode of teaching. First, in "comprehensive brevity"—a quality indispensable to all elementary works—the rules and examples are divided, broken up, and scattered into portions so far apart, that before the pupil has arrived at the end of the rule and examples, the commencement is not unfrequently forgotten: 2nd, in "educational permanency"—a quality of paramount necessity to the pupil,—the mode adopted of giving the rules in English only, and in isolated paragraphs or sentences, often too loosely paraphrased—is not calculated to leave a permanent impression on the memory: which requires the objects presented for its retention, in a form more tangible as well as more impressible.

Here the superiority of Latin Rules is manifest,—presenting *within the shortest space, in regular Hexameter verse, and in form calculated to leave an indelible impression on the mind of the Learner*

---

* Enumerated in the course of the work.

—all that is requisite for the clear understanding of each rule and its various exceptions.

To attempt in any other way to teach Latin Prosody soundly, and with a view to permanent retention, must, in the vast majority of cases, ever prove abortive: and in the course of the compiler's experience, for more than twenty years as a teacher of classics, as well in Europe as in America, he has never met a good Prosodian, who had not been taught in this manner—by rules brief but comprehensive, written in Latin Hexameter verse, with (or without) a translation in the vernacular.

In the compilation of the present work, the author has taken care, to adapt it to either method—that of teaching Latin Prosody by Latin rules only or by English: whereas the translation appended to each rule will suit the purpose of those who may prefer the latter; so that the advocates of either can adopt that of his choice, or, following the *crede-experto* advice of the compiler, make use of both united.

The plan of the work is, nevertheless, different from any hitherto published; and, as it is believed, an improvement on all preceding compilations, whether in Europe or in America. Wishing to render it as easy and as intelligible as possible to the tender capacity of youth, as well as to raise it by regular gradation to the capacity and comprehension of the more advanced, the compiler has,—after giving each rule in Latin Hexameter verse, followed in a sufficiently literal translation,—1st, exemplified not only the rule, but its various exceptions and observations by *single words* only, without at this stage embarrassing the student by examples in Hexameter or any other kind of verse; 2ndly, he has given *Promiscuous Examples*—still by single words—for exercising the learner in the rule under consideration as well as on all the preceding rules without anticipating any subsequent; 3rdly, he has, for each rule, exception and observation, given *Examples in Composition*, or in combination of feet—Hexameter* throughout (save in two or three unavoidable instances); and 4thly, after the pupil will have, in this manner, gone through not only the *Rules of Quantity*, but the *Figures of Prosody*, and the sections treating of *Metre, Versification*, and *the Different Kinds of Verse*, the compiler has given at the end a SUPPLEMENT or RECAPITULATION, containing Examples of *all* the *Rules of Quantity, Figures of Prosody*, and *Different Kinds of Verse*, requisite to test the pupil's progress at the conclusion of the work.

In the text, little has been admitted not pertinent to the rule under consideration; in order that the student having nothing to unsettle his eye or distract his attention, may afterwards more profit-

* Any other species, until the pupil had read and studied the sections on *Metre, Versification*, and *Different Kinds of Verse*, being deemed anticipatory and irrelevant.

ably peruse the illustrations, derivations, or remarks thrown into the notes in the margin. By the time the pupil has gone regularly through this work, if carefully directed by a judicious teacher, it may with all confidence be asserted that he will have acquired a better, more extended, and enduring knowledge of the subject than by any other compilation extant. And in order that this little treatise may, in every point of view, be regarded as complete, STIRLING's excellent *System of Rhetoric* has been appended; leaving nothing to be desired in the formation of the perfect Prosodian.

The object of the compiler has been to collect within the shortest space, what his own experience had long felt to be a desideratum— *A Compendious but Complete System of Latin Prosody;* embracing all that is necessary to impart a correct knowledge of this elegant branch of classical study;—in one word, to constitute *the easiest, the best, the most concise, and yet the most comprehensive Latin Prosody ever published.*

How far he has succeeded, remains with the public voice to determine.

# PREFACE TO THE SECOND EDITION.

The sale of one large Edition and the urgent demand for another, in little more than twelve months, may be regarded as ample criteria not only of the popularity of the work itself but also of the growing taste of the public mind for a more accurate cultivation of Classical studies.

In order to render it still further deserving of a patronage rarely awarded in this or indeed in any country to a work of the kind, the volume has been carefully revised and corrected throughout;—many false quantities, which had escaped observation in the first edition, have been rectified, and some useful additions incorporated.

By the experienced Teacher, the elegant Scholar, and the curious Student, these improvements will, it is presumed, be duly appreciated.

To the Heads of Colleges, Schools, and Academies, by whom his *Complete System of Latin Prosody* has been introduced and adopted in their respective Institutions, the Author tenders his thanks, and hopes that the care manifested in the preparation of this second Edition,—now stereotyped, will be received as a proof of no illaudable anxiety to deserve a continuance of a patronage already so liberally extended.

PATRICK S. CASSERLY.

*New York: November,* 1846.

☞ A Second Part on *Latin Versification*, comprehending a plain and easy method of constructing Latin Hexameters, Pentamenters, Iambics, and other kinds of verse, is in course of preparation. A copious Index to both First and Second Parts will be given at the conclusion.

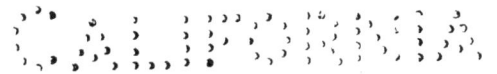

# PROSODY.

## SECTION I.

Prosody* is that part of grammar, which treats of —1st. *Accent;* 2d. *The Length or Quantity of Syllables,* 3d. *The correct Pronunciation of Words:* 4th. *The different species of Verse;* and 5th. *The Rules of Metrical Composition.*

Letters are divided into vowels and consonants. The vowels are six: A, E, I, O, U, Y. From these are formed nine diphthongs: Æ, AI, AU, EI, EU, Œ, YI, OI, UI; as in *Præmium, Maia, Aurum, Hei, Europa, Pœna, Harpyia, Troia, Quis.* Some of these, however, are not, strictly speaking, proper diphthongs.

Consonants are divided into mutes and semivowels. The mutes are eight: B, C, D, G, K, P, Q, T. The semivowels are likewise eight: F, L, M, N, R, S, X, Z. Of these semivowels, four, viz. L, M, N, R, are called liquids, because they easily flow into, or, as it were, *liquify* with, other letters† or sounds. F before the liquids L and R has the force of a mute. Two of the semivowels are also called *double letters,* X and Z: the X being equivalent to CS, GS, or KS; and Z having the force of DS or SD. The letter H is not regarded in prosody as a letter or consonant, but as a mere aspirate or breathing. The letters I or J, and U or V placed before vowels, are regarded as consonants: as, *Janua, Jocus, Vita, Vultus.*

---

* From two Greeks words πρός, "according to," and ᾠδή, "song or melody."
† With the mutes, for instance, when preceding them in the same syllable.

U generally loses its force after Q, and sometimes after G and S; as *Aqua, Lingua, Suadeo*:—being, in some measure, absorbed by, or liquified into, the letter preceding. It sometimes, however, retains its force; as, *Exiguus*.

## SECTION II.

### OF ACCENT.*

Accents in Latin were little marks placed over words to direct or distinguish the tone or inflection of the voice in pronunciation. During the flourishing state of the language, these tones or inflections were not marked in books; because the Romans, to whom usage and practice had made them at once both natural and familiar, did not require the aid of any such accentual guidance to the proper enunciation of their native tongue:—*Exempla eorum tradi scripto non possunt*—says Quintilian. They were invented in after times to fix the pronunciation and render its acquisition easy to foreigners.

Of these accents there were three; viz., the *acute*, marked thus (´),—the *grave*, thus (`)—and the *circumflex*, thus (^); being the junction of the other two. The *acute* was also called ἄρσις, because it elevates the syllable, as, *dóminus*; the *grave*—which is in reality the absence or privation of accent—is called θέσις, because it sinks or depresses the syllable; as *doctè*;† while the *circumflex* both elevates and depresses it: as, *amâre*.

These accents being invented solely to mark the tone, elevation or depression of the voice, were not regarded as signs of the quantity of syllables whether long or short. In modern typography they have—an occasional

---

* From *accentum*, wh. fr. *accino*, "I sing to," or "in concert with."
† The last syllable of Latin words (in dissyllables, &c.,) never admits the *acute* or *circumflex*, unless for the sake of distinction between words similar in orthography but different in meaning; as *ergò*, "on account of," to distinguish it from *érgo*, "therefore;" or *ponè*, "behind," from *póne*, the imperative mood of *póno*. The *grave* is however supposed to be placed over the last syllable of all words, dissyllables, &c., not thus excepted.

use of the *circumflex* excepted—been long generally omitted; yet as the reading or the recitation of the Latin language is, (or at least ought to be,) in some degree, regulated by their influence whether marked or not, it it has been considered necessary to give a few short rules for their application.

### MONOSYLLABLES :—

1. If long by nature, are always supposed to have a *circumflex;* as, *flôs, spês, ôs (oris), â, î :*—if short by nature or long by position, they are considered to have an *acute ;* as, *vír, ós, (ossis,) fáx, méns.*

### DISSYLLABLES :—

2. Having the first syllable long by nature and the second short, have the *circumflex* on the first; as, *Rôma, flôris, lûna :*—but if the first syllable is short by nature or long by position, it takes the *acute ;* as, *hómo, párens, ínsons.*

### POLYSYLLABLES :

3. With the penultimate long and the ultimate short, require a *circumflex* on the former; as, *Românus, Imperâtor, Justiniânus.* If both penultimate and ultimate be long, the penultimate takes the *acute ;* as, *paréntes, amavérunt :*—if the penultimate be short, then the antepenultimate\* has the *acute ;* as, *dóminus, hómines, Virgílius.*

EXCEPTION. Words compounded with *enclitics,* such

---

\* No mark or accent in Latin can be placed farther back than the antepenultimate; because if three, four, or more syllables were to follow the accent,—as, *pérficeremus, Cónstantinopolis*—they would come so huddled or confusedly heaped on one another, as to be undistinguishable in cadence, by the ear: which, as Cicero remarks, cannot well determine the accent unless by the last three syllables of a word, in the same way as it determines the harmony of a period, by the last three words in the sentence.

as the particles, *que, ne, ve,* and some prepositions, as *cum,* most commonly throw the accent on the last syllable preceding the adjunct particle or preposition; as, *ámat,*—when followed by an enclitic—becomes *amátque,* so also, *lachrymánsve, probétne; nóbis* becomes *nobíscum, quibúscum,* &c.

OBSERVATION. It may, nevertheless, admit of some doubt, if this exception can hold good, unless where the penultimate is long; for instance in this line from Ovid—

*Prónaque cum spectent animalia cætera terram—*

the accent must fall on the first, not on the last, syllable of *Próna,* contrary to the commonly received opinion on the power of the enclitics to attract the accent. Various similar examples abound in the classics.

The foregoing are the only rules for accentuation, as laid down by the old Roman grammarians, that have reached our times, and which can, with any regard to classical accuracy or elegance, be safely recommended to the attention of the student. As to the barbarous practice of attempting to anglicise the venerable and majestic languages of Greece and Rome, by reading them according to the laws and principles of modern English accent, it is so absurd in the inception, so subversive of all beauty, melody, and accuracy in recitation of the classic authors, and so utterly destructive of all distinction between accent and quantity, as to deserve universal reprobation.

## SECTION III.

### OF THE QUANTITY OF SYLLABLES.

Quantity is distinct from accent though not inconsistent with it. The former denotes the period of time occupied in pronouncing a syllable; the latter is used to signify a peculiar tone, as above described, by which one syllable in a word is distinguished from the rest. The one is length or continuance, whether long or short, the other is elevation or depression of sound, or both.*

The length or quantity of a syllable then is the duration of time occupied in pronouncing it. A syllable is either *short*, *long*, or *common*. The length or quantity of syllables is marked, as in the word *ămālŏ;* of which the first syllable is short, the second long, and the third common. A *short* syllable is pronounced rapidly; as, *concĭdo, lĕgĕrĕ*. A *long* syllable is pronounced slowly; as, *concīdo, sedāre*. Hence, in the language of prosodians, a short syllable is said to have *one time* and a long syllable, *two times*. A *common* or *doubtful* syllable is that

---

* In the great majority of the Classical Institutions throughout the United States, it is to be regretted, that the practice of reading the ancient authors according to accent alone—not, however, the accent of the old Romans, but *modern English accent!*—instead of by quantity, prevails to an extent likely to prove injurious to the best interests of elegant literature. What, for instance, can be more irreconcilable to classical purity of taste or correctness, than to find in some of the most popular Latin grammars of the country, rules laid down in which the pupil is gravely instructed to pronounce the *i* in *parietes* and *mulieres* LONG! because "it is accented and comes before another vowel!"—and the *i* in *fides* also LONG! because "it comes before a single consonant"! and this, although he (the pupil) must then, or shortly know, that, in accordance with the very first rule in his prosody, "A Vowel before a Vowel is short," and by another rule that "Derivatives must follow the quantity of their Primitives;" and that in the entire *Corpus Poetarum*, he will not find a single instance in which the *i* in any of these words is otherwise than *short?* Is it then a matter of wonder to find so few classical scholars in the United States taught in this preposterous manner, who can read a page of Homer or Virgil prosodially? Their incompetence is the inevitable result of the perverted mode of teaching adopted *ab limine:* inconsiderately endeavoring to reduce the laws of a dead language which have been ascertained and fixed for centuries to those of a living and variable language whose very accentuation and pronunciation are yet in a state of transition; neither unchangeably fixed nor unalterably ascertained. Instead of rationally teaching their pupils to read the exquisitely beautiful and wonderfully metrical language of Greece or of Rome agreeably to its own laws and principles, as well of quantity as of accent, most of our cisatlantic Professors endeavor with more than Procrustean ingenuity (qu. cruelty?) to stretch or shorten it to the shifting standard of their own immature and imperfect vernacular! Would that these gentlemen were more observant of the advice given by the great Roman orator —: Atque ut Latinè loquamur, non solum videndum est, ut et verba efferamus ea quæ nemo jure reprehendat; et ea sic et casibus, et temporibus, et genere, et *numero* conservemus, ut nequid perturbatum ac discrepans aut præposterum sit; sed etiam lingua, et spiritus, et vocis sonus est ipse moderandus.—*De Orat.* lib. iii.

which in poetry is sometimes *long* and sometimes *short;* as, *ĭtalus* or *ītalus, Papȳrus* or *Papy̆rus, Vaticānus* or *Vaticănus,* &c.

The quantity of syllables is determined either by established rules or the authority of the poets. The last syllable of a word is called the *ultimate;* the last but one, the *penultimate;* the last but two, the *antepenultimate;* and the last but three, the *præ-antepenultimate.*

### RULE I.

### *A Vowel before a Vowel.*

Vocalem breviant, alia subeunte, Latini.
Produc, ni sequitur R, *f ĭo*, et nomina quintæ
Quæ geminos casus, E longo, assumunt in *-ēi,*
Verum E corripiunt *fĭdĕi*que, *spĕi*que, *rĕi*que.
*-ĭus* commune est vati, tamen excipe *alīus,*
Quod Crasis tardat ; *Pompēi* et cætera produc,
Et primæ patrium cum sese solvit in *-āï ;*
Protrahiturque *ēheu,* sed *ĭo* variatur et *ŏhe.*
Nomina Græcorum certâ sine lege vagantur :
Multa etenim longis, ceu *Dīus, Dīa, Thalīa,*
Quædam autem brevibus, veluti *Symphŏnĭa,* gaudent ;
Quædam etiam variant, veluti *Dīana, Dĭana.*

A vowel before another vowel or a diphthong, is short ; as, *pŭer, patrĭæ:* or before *h* followed by a vowel ; as, *nĭhil.*

EXCEPTION 1. A vowel before a vowel is long in all the tenses of *fio ;* as, *fīebam;* unless where the vowel is followed by *r*, (or rather by *er*); as, *fĭerem.*\*

EXCEP. 2. The genitives and datives singular of the fifth declension make *e* long before *i ;* as, *diēi :* except

---

\* Carey in his translation of the Latin rule says—"when *r* follows, the *i* is usually short ;—and adduces five decisive examples where it is long; so that it may, in some degree, be regarded as common. In no species of Dactylic verse can it be ever found long.

the *e* in *spĕi, rĕi, fidĕi*. In the last two words, it is sometimes ong; as, *rēi, fidēi*.

Excep. 3. Genitives in *ius* have the *i* long in prose, but common in poetry; as, *unĭus:* the word *alterĭus* however has the *i* always short; *alīus* always long—being formed by Crasis\* from *aliius*.

Excep. 4. Proper names, as, *Cāius, Pompēius*, have the vowel *a* or *e* long before *i:* the *a* is also long in the old genitives and datives, *aulāï, terrāï*.

Excep. 5. In *ŏhe* and *Dĭana*, the vowel in the first syllable is common: in *ēheu* and *Io* [a proper name] it is long; but *ĭo* the interjection, follows the general rule.

Excep. 6. In many other words derived from the Greek, a vowel though immediately followed by another, is long; as, *Orīon, āër*.

☞ Foreign or barbarous words introduced into the Latin language, are not subject to any invariable rule. Prudentius lengthens the first *a* in *Baal*, while Sedulius shortens it. Sidonius lengthens the penultimate vowel in *Abraham*, while Arator shortens it. Christian poets also make the *a* before *e* in *Israel, Michael, Raphael*, &c., &c., sometimes long, and sometimes short.

EXAMPLES FOR PRACTICE—BY SINGLE WORDS.

*On Rule:*—Audïisse, aureæ, mĭhi:—*On Exceptions:* 1. fīunt, fīerent; 2. specīei, diēi; 3. totĭus, nullĭus; 4. Vultēïus, Grāïus, pictāï; 5. ŏhe, ēheu; 6. Clīo, chorĕa.†

EXAMPLES IN COMPOSITION.

Rule—*Conscĭa mens recti famæ mendacĭa ridet.* Ovid.
*Musa, mĭhi causas memora; quo numine læso.* Virg.
Exc. 1. *Omnia jam fīent, fīeri quæ posse negabam.* Ovid.
2. *Nunc adeo, melior quoniam pars acta diēi.* Virg.

\* Derived from κρᾶσις (fr. κεράω, or κεράννυμι), "a mingling,"—in grammar—"a blending of two letters into one." † The *e* in *chorea* is common.

Exc. 3. *Navibus, infandum! amissis, unīus ob iram.* Virg.
4. *Aulāï in medio libabant pocula Bacchi.* Id.
5. *Exercet Dīana choros, quam mille secutæ.* Id.
6. *Pars pedibus plaudunt chorĕas et carmina dicunt.* Id.

### RULE II.

### *Of Diphthongs and Contracted Syllables.*

Omnis diphthongus, contractaque syllaba longa est.
*Præ* brevis est, si compositum vocalibus anteit.

Every diphthong and syllable formed by contraction are long; as, *aurum, cōgo* [from *co-ago*].

Excep. *Præ* immediately before a vowel in a compound word, is generally short; as, *prǣ acutus*.

#### EXAMPLES FOR PRACTICE, BY SINGLE WORDS.

*On Rule:*—Æneas, cœlum, nēmo [from nehemo]:—
*On Excep.* Prǣ-ustus, prǣ-eunt.

*Promiscuous Examples on this and the preceding Rule.*
Ænēas [2, 1 Gr.], vitæ [2], meridīēi [1, 1], fīemus [1], āonides [Gr. 1.], prælīa [2, 1], fūit [1], prǣ-eo [2], spēi [1], jūnior—from jŭĕnior, wh. fr. jŭvĕnior—[2.]

#### EXAMPLES IN COMPOSITION.

Rule. *En Priamus! sunt hîc etiam sua prǣmia laudi.* Vir.
  *Bis gravidos cōgunt fœtus, duo tempora messis.* Id.
Ex. *Jamque novi prǣeunt fasces, nova purpura fulget.* Clau.

### RULE III.

### *Of Position.*

Vocalis longa est, si consona bina sequatur,
Aut duplex, aut *I* vocalibus interjectum.

A vowel before two consonants in the same word or syllable, is long by position;* as, *tērra.* The same effect

---

* That is, by being *so* situated, although naturally short.

is produced by two consonants in different words; as, *pēr me:* also when the vowel comes before a double consonant; [x or z;] as, *jŭdex, gāza:* or before the letter *j*; as, *mājor, hūjus.*\*

Excep. 1. The compounds of *jugum* have the *i* short before *j*; as *bĭjugus, quadrĭjugus.*

Excep. 2. A short vowel at the end of a word, preceding another word beginning with *x* or *z*, remains short; as, *litoră Xerxes; nemorosă Zacynthos.*

Excep. 3. A short vowel at the end of a word, preceding another vowel beginning with *sc, sm, sp, sq, st, scr,* &c., sometimes remains short, but is generally made long; as, *undĕ sciat; liberă sponte; sæpĕ stylum—nefariā scripta; complerē spatium; gelidā stabula.*

Observation. The letter *h* not being regarded in prosody as a letter, has no influence, either in the beginning, middle or end of a word, on the preceding short vowel; as, *ădhuc:*—nor at the beginning of a word, does it like a consonant, preserve the final vowel of the preceding word from elision; as, *Icare haberes*—where the final *e* of *Icare* is elided.

EXAMPLES FOR PRACTICE, BY SINGLE WORDS.

*On Rule:*—Mōrs, rāptum, tēndēns, āt pius; pāx, horizon — *On Excep.* Bĭjugis, jurā Zaleucus, Agĭlĕ studium.

*Promiscuous Examples.*—Īnstaūrat [3, 2], īntonŭit [3, 1], hūjus [3], posŭīsse [1, 3], Thalīa [Gr. 1], facĭēi [1], erāt mĭhi [3, 1], fĭeri [1], pērfidĭa [3, 1], gaūdia [2, 1], ēxpērtum [3, 3].

\* Not because *j* is a double consonant, or indeed in this situation any consonant at all, but because joined with the preceding vowel, it constitutes a diphthong, both in pronunciation and quantity. Moreover, many words of this formation, which were originally written and pronounced in three syllables, as *hu-i-us,* coalescing into dissyllables, the first syllable became a diphthong. J in any other situation is regarded as a consonant, and appears to have been pronounced by the Romans like y in English.

### EXAMPLES IN COMPOSITION.

Rule— *Sācra suōsque tibi cōmmēndāt Trōja penates.* Virg.
*Sūb juga jām Serēs, jam bărbarus īsset Arāxes.* Luc.
Exc. 1. *Centum quadrĭjugos agitabo ad flumina currus.* Vir.
 2. *Jam medio apparet fluctu nemorosŭ Zacynthos.* Id.
 3. *Sæpĕ stylum vertas, iterum quæ digna legi sint.* Hor.
 *Ferte citi ferrum ; date telā ; scandite muros.* Vir.
Obser. *Oro, siquis ădhuc precibus locus, exue mentem.* Id.
 *Partem opere in tanto, sineret dolor Icare\* haberes.* Id.

### RULE IV.

*Of the Mute and Liquid, or Weak Position.*†

Si mutam liquidamque simul brevis una præivet,
Contrahit orator, variant in carmine vates.

A short vowel preceding a mute and a liquid—both in the following syllable—is common in poetry, but short in prose; as, *ăgris* and *āgris; pătrem* and *pātrem; volŭcris* and *volūcris.*

OBSERV.—This rule requires the concurrence of three circumstances; viz., 1st, the vowel must be naturally short; thus because the *a* in *păter* is short by nature, the *a* in *pătris* is common,‡ in accordance with the rule; but the *a* in *mātris, ācris,* is always long, being long by nature in *māter* and *ācer;*—2d, the mute must precede the liquid; as, *pharetra;* because if the liquid stand before the mute, the vowel preceding though naturally short, is always long; as, *fĕrt, fĕrtis;*—3d, both

---

\* E in *Icare* is elided.

† *Debilis Positio,* as the position formed by a mute and a liquid, is called by Prosodians.

‡ The lengthening of the vowel in poetry may be rendered more familiar to the youthful student, by causing him to pronounce the words in separate syllables; thus *păt-ris, intĕg-ra, pharĕt-ram;* so that the halt of the voice produced by throwing the consonants into different syllables, must be counted into the time of the preceding syllable and will consequently render it long.

mute and liquid must belong to the same syllable; as, *medio-cris, mulie-bris :* because if the mute and liquid belong to different syllables, the preceding short vowel necessarily becomes long, by position; as, *ăb-luo, quamŏb-rem.*

### EXAMPLES FOR PRACTICE, BY SINGLE WORDS.

*On Rule*—Tenĕbræ, locŭples, tonĭtrua ;—in *poetry.*
*On Observation*—mātres, fērtis, ārtis.
*Promiscuous Examples*—Sĕd dīxit [3, 3], rēspūblica [3, 3], vīrgineæ [3, 1, 2], mājor [3], ēheū [1, 2], Cālliopēa [3, 1, Gr.] pătris [4], *Proteū* [2,] mălo—fr. măgis vŏlo—[2], aūreum [2, 1], Arāxes [3], ŏhe [1], præōptat [2, 3].

NOTE. A short vowel at the end of a word frequently remains short, although the next word should begin with two or three consonants ; as, *fastidirĕ : Strabonem.*

### EXAMPLES IN COMPOSITION.

Rule—*Et primo similis volŭcri, mox vera volŭcris.* Ovid.
*Natum ante ora pătris, pătrem qui obtruncat ad aras.* Vir.
Obser. *Pars leves humero pharĕtras, et pectore summo.* Id.
*Dixit, et in sylvam pennis āblata refugit.* Id.
Note. *Linquimus, insani ridentes præmiă scribæ.* Hor.

### RULE V.

### *Of Derivative Words.*

Derivata, patris naturam, verba sequuntur.
*Mōbilis* et *fōmes, lāterna* ac *rēgula, sēdes,*
Quanquam orta è brevibus, gaudent producere primam :
Corripiuntur *ărista, vădum, sŏpor* atque *lŭcerna,*
Nata licet longis. Usus te plura docebit.

Words derived from others usually follow the nature or quantity of the words, whence they are formed ; as, ănĭmosus from ănĭmus, [but ănĭmatus fr. ănĭmá,*] făcundus from fări, īrăcundus, from the obsolete verb īro, īrāre.

Excep. 1. Mōbilis, fōmes, lāterna, rēgula, and sēdes have their first syllable long, although derived from words which have the same syllable short; viz., mŏveo, fŏveo, lăteo, rĕgo, and sĕdeo.

Excep. 2. Ărista, vădum, sŏpor and lŭcerna have their first syllable short although derived from āreo, vādo, sōpio, and lūceo in which the first syllable is long. Familiarity with the classic writers will furnish more numerous examples of these apparent anomalies.†

Note. The entire class of verbs in urio called *Desideratives*, have the u short, although derived from the future participle in ūrus, of which the penultima is invariably long; as, esŭrit, cœnatŭrit, scriptŭrit: but indeed the derivative and compound words, that deviate from the quantity of their primitives, are too many to be enumerated and too unconnected to be reduced into classes.

### EXAMPLES BY SINGLE WORDS.

*On Rule*—Lībido [fr. lĭbet], lĭcentia [fr. lĭcet], lĕgebam [fr. lĕgo], lēgeram, lēgissem [fr. lēgi]:—*On Excep.* 1. Mōbilis [fr. mŏveo], sēdes [fr. sĕdeo]:—*Excep.* 2. Vădum [fr. vādo], lŭcerna [fr. lūceo]:—*On Note.* Partŭrio [ūrus].

*Promiscuous Examples.*—Fīnitimus—fr. fīnis—[5], mōlēstus—fr. mōles—[5, 3] sălūbris—fr. sălus, salūtis [5, 4], genĕtrīx [4, 3], Æææ [2], Eŭbœa [2], lĭtanīa [5,

---

* The distinction between *anĭmus* and *anima*, although both derived from the same Greek origin, should be kept in view by the learner. *Sapimus animo; fruimur anima; sine animo, anima est debilis.*

† Many of these are, however, only apparent anomalies; perhaps it might be said so of all, were we better acquainted with the early state of the Latin language and the forgotten dialects on which it was founded. Thus, instead of saying, that *fomes* comes from *fŏveo*, we should derive it from the supine *fŏtum ;* formed by contraction and syncope from *fŏvĭtum ;*—so also, *mobilis* should be derived not from *mŏveo* but from *mōtum ;* formed in like manner from *mŏvĭtum :* and so of others

1.], ĕxĭmĭæ [3, 5, 1, 3], cŏhærēnt [1, 2, 3], cŭrūlis—fr. cŭcŭrri, *perf. of* cūrro—[5].

### EXAMPLES IN COMPOSITION.

Rule—*Non formosus erat, sed erat fācundus, Ulysses.* Ov.
Exc. 1. *Sēdibus optatis gemina super arbore sidunt.* Virg.
Exc. 2. *Alituum pecudumque genus, sōpor altus habebat.* Id.
Note. *Partŭriunt montes, nascetur ridiculus mus.* Hor.

### RULE VI.

### *Of Compound Words.*

Legem simplicium retinent composta suorum,
Vocalem licet aut dipthongum syllaba mutet.
*Dejĕro* corripies cum *pejĕro* et *innŭba;* necnon
*Pronŭba; fatidĭcum* et socios cum *semisŏpitus*
Queis etiam *nihĭlum*, cum *cognĭtus, agnĭtus*, hæret
Longam *imbēcillus*, verbumque *ambĭtus* amabit.

Compound words usually retain the quantity of the simple words whence they are formed; as, *perlĕgŏ, admŏnet, consŏnans* have the middle syllable short, agreeably to the quantity of the corresponding syllable of their primitives, *lĕgo, mŏnet, sŏnans;* while *perlēgi, remōtus, ablātus*, have the penultima long, because it is long in *lēgi, mōtus, lātus*, whence derived.

The quantity of the simple words is generally preserved in the compounds, although the vowels be changed in the derivation; as, *concīdo, occīdo* from *cădo; elĭgo, selĭgo* from *lĕgo; excīdo, occīdo* from *cædo; allīdo* from *lædo; obēdio* from *audio*, &c., &c.

EXCEPTIONS. *Dejĕro, pejĕro*, from *jūro; innŭba, pronŭba*, from *nūbo; fatidĭcus, maledĭcus, causidĭcus, veridĭcus*, from *dīco: semisŏpitus* from *sōpitus; nihĭlum* from *ne hilum: cognĭtum, agnĭtum*, from *nōtum; imbēcillus* from *băculus* or *băcillum; ambĭtus* the participle from *ambĭo* has *i* long, but the substantives *ambĭtus* and *ambĭtio* make it short.*

Note. *Connŭbium* from *nūbo* is generally reckoned common.

### EXAMPLES BY SINGLE WORDS.

*Rule.* Cohĭbet [hăbet], imprŏbus [prŏbus], perjūrus [jŭs, jūris], oblītum [oblĭno], oblītus [oblīvīscor], inīquus [æquus]. *Excep.* Causidĭcus, maledĭcus, [dīco], cognĭtum [nōtum], &c., &c. *Note.* Connŭbium, [nūbo].

*Promiscuous Examples.* Dēfĕro—fr. dē and fĕro—[6,6], perhĭbeo—fr. hăbeo [6], mācero—fr. măcer—[5], nŏta—fr. nōtu—[5], cўcni [4], tērrēnt [3], præĕūnte [2, 1, 3], dīs, for dīis—[2], specĭēi [1, 1], dĕæ [1, 2].

### EXAMPLES IN COMPOSITION.

*Rule.*—*Multa renascentur, quæ jam cecĭdere; cădentque.* Hor.
*Quandoquidem dăta sunt ipsis quoque fata sepulcris.* Juv.
*Exc. Et Bellona manet te pronŭba; nec face tantum.* Virg.
*Note. Connŭbio jungam stabili, propriamque dicabo.* Id.

### RULE VII.

*Of Preterites of two Syllables.*

Præterita assumunt primam dissyllaba longam.
*Sto, do, scindo, fero* rapiunt, *bibo, findo,* priores.

Preterperfect tenses of two syllables have the first syllable long; as, *vēni*,† *vīdi, vīci, fūgi, crēvi,* &c.

---

* *Ambĭtus* should not be derived from *ambĭo* but from the supine *ambĭtum;* while *ambĭtus* and *ambĭtio* must be formed from the supine *ambĭtum,* from the obsolete verb *amb-eo, ambĭtum.* In this manner, can the curious student be taught to explain many of the deviations from the rule.

† Agreeably to the theory of many able writers on Philology, most verbs which change the short vowel of the present tense into long *e* of the perfect, had originally a reduplicating perfect; thus *pango* [*pago*] in the present, makes *pepĭgi* in the perfect; so also *video* made *vivĭdi,* by syncope, *vīĭdi,* and by crasis, *vĭdi; fūgio,* made *fŭfŭgi,* by syncope, *fŭŭgi,* and by crasis, *fūgi; venio* made *vĕvĕni,* by syncope, *vĕēni,* and by crasis, *vēni,* &c., &c. Other verbs having a long vowel in the perfect, underwent a different formation; thus, *rideo* made *rīdsi,* by syncope, *rīsi; mitto* made *mīttsi,* by syncope, *mīsi,* &c., &c.

## REDUPLICATING PRETERITES. 15

Exceptions. *Stĕti, dĕdi, scĭdi,* [fr. *scindo*] *tŭli, bĭbi* and *fĭdi,* [fr. *findo*] have the first syllable short.

Note. *Abscīdi* from *cædo* has the penultima long; but *abscĭdit* fr. *scindo* has it short.

### EXAMPLES BY SINGLE WORDS.

*Rule.* Mīsi, vīdi, jēci. *Excep.* Stĕti, tŭli, bĭbi.
*Promiscuous Examples.*—Pērvīcet [3, 7], cōntŭlerūnt [3, 7, 3], dīxīsti [3, 3], ĕlĕgīa [fr. Gr. ἐλἐγεἰα,—5, 5, 1], fīeri [1], spĕi [1], bĭberūnt [7, 3].

### EXAMPLES IN COMPOSITION.

*Rule. Cur aliquid vīdi? cur noxia luminà fēci?* Ovid.
*Exc. Cui mater media sese tŭlit obvia sylva.* Virg.
Note. *Abscīdit nostra multum sors invida laudi.* Lucan.

### RULE VIII.

*Of Preterites doubling the first Syllable.*

Præteritum geminans primam breviabit utramque;
Ut *pario, pĕpĕri,* vetet id nisi consona bina;
*Cædo cĕcīdit* habet, longâ, ceu *pedo,* secundâ.

Preterperfect tenses doubling their first syllable, make both first and second syllable short; as, *pĕpĕri, tĕtĭgi, dĭdĭci, cĕcĭni,* &c., &c.

Excep. 1. The second syllable frequently becomes long by position, the first remaining short according to the rule; as, *mŏmōrdi, tĕtēndi, cŭcūrri,* &c.

Excep. 2. *Cĕcīdi* from *cædo,* and *pĕpēdi* from *pēdo* have the second long.

### EXAMPLES BY SINGLE WORDS,

*Rule.* Cĕcĭni, tĕtĭgi, pĕpŭli, cĕcĭni. *Excep.* 1. Fĕfĕlli, cŭcūrri. *Excep.* 2. Cĕcīdi.

*Promiscuous Examples.* Nōvi [7], dĕdīsti [7, 3], ăbscĭdit [3, 7], mājores [3], vīxīsse [3], licŭīsset [1, 3], stĕteram [7], pĕpŭli [8, 8], Arīon [Gr. 1], sēdes—fr. sĕdeo—[5], injĭcio—fr. jăcio—[6, 1].

### EXAMPLES IN COMPOSITION.

Rule. *Tityre, te patulæ cĕcĭni sub tegmine fagi.* Virg.
*Litora, quæ cornu pĕpŭlit Saturnus equino.* Val. Flac.
Exc. 1. *Stella facem ducens multa cum luce cŭcūrrit.* Vir.
Exc. 2. *Ebrius ac petulans, qui nullum forte cĕcĭdit.* Juv.

### RULE IX.

*Of Supines of two Syllables.*

Cuncta supina volunt primam dissyllaba longam.
At *reor* et *cieo, sero* et *ire, sino*que *lino*que.
*Do, queo,* et orta *ruo,* breviabunt rite priores.

Supines of two syllables, as well as those parts of the verb derived therefrom, have the first syllable long; as, *vīsum, mōtum; vīsus, vīsurus; mōtus, mōturus,* &c.

EXCEP. 1. *Rătum* from *reor, cĭtum* from *cieo, sătum* from *sero, ĭtum* from *eo, sĭtum* from *sino, lĭtum*\* from *lino, dătum* from *do, quĭtum* from *queo,* and *rŭtum* from *ruo*— [with *fŭtum* from the obsolete *fuo,* whence *fŭturus,*] have the first syllable short.

NOTE. Although *cĭtum* from *cieo* of the second conjugation has the first syllable short—whence *cĭtus, concĭtus, excĭtus,* &c.;—*Cītum* from *cio* of the fourth conjugation, has the first syllable long: whence, also, *cītus, accītus, concītus,* &c., &c. Some Prosodians would have *statum* common; but *stătum* or *stītum* comes from *sto* or *sisto* of the third conjugation, while *stātum* is of the first.

### EXAMPLES BY SINGLE WORDS.

*Rule.* Mōtum, vīsum, flētum. *Excep.* Rătum, stătum, ĭtum, obrŭtum, cĭtum [fr. cieo].

---

\* *Oblĭtus,* "smeared," from *lino,* must be distinguished from *oblītus,* "having forgotten," which comes from *obliviscor.*

*Note.* Cĭtum [fr. cio] cĭtus, incĭtus.

*Promiscuous Examples.* Ātrum—fr. āter—[4], āëra [1], sapiēns [1, 3], laŭdānt [2, 3], solĭus [1], cædo [2], pĕpĕrit [8], stătus [9], jēcĭsti [7, 3] dĕdit, [7], tŭtŭdi [8], ĭturus [9].

### EXAMPLES IN COMPOSITION.

Rule. *Lūsum it Mæcenas, dormitum ego Virgiliusque.*
Hor.
*Nascitur et casus abies vīsura marinos.*   Virg.
Exc. 1. *Cui dătus hærebam custos cursusque regebam.* Id.
Note. *Altior insurgens et cursu concĭtus heros.*   Id.
*Rupta quies populis, stratisque excĭta juventus.* Luc.
*Tunc res immenso placuit stătura labore.*   Id.

### RULE X.

### Of Polysyllabic Supines.

*Utum* producunt polysyllaba quæque supina.
*-ivi* præterito semper producitur *-ītum.*
Cætera corripias in *-ĭtum* quæcunque supina.

Supines in *utum* [and also *atum* and *etum*] of more than two syllables, as well as all parts of the verb derived therefrom, have the penultima long; as, *solūtum, argūtum, indūtum;* [*amātum, delētum.*]

Excep. 1. Supines in *itum* from preterites in *ivi* are, in like manner long; as, *petītum, quæsītum, cupītum.*

Excep. 2. Supines in *itum* from any other preterites, have the penultima short; as, *monĭtum, tacĭtum, cubĭtum.*\*

Note. This exception does not include polysyllabic compounds from supines of two syllables: whereas these compounds retain the quantity of the supines whence they had been formed; as, *obītum* from *ītum, abdĭtum* fr. *dătum, insĭtum* fr. *sătum*, &c.; except *cognĭtum* and *agnĭtum* fr. *nōtum.*

---

\* *Recensĭtum* usually given as an exception, may be derived from *censio, censivi*, and not from *censeo, censivi.*

## EXAMPLES BY SINGLE WORDS.

*Rule.* Solūtum, indūtum, argūtum. *Excep.* 1. Audĭtum, polĭtum, cupĭtum. *Excep.* 2. Credĭtum, agnĭtum, cubĭtum. *Note.* Condĭtum, insĭtum, reddĭtum.

*Promiscuous Examples.* Cōndĭtum—fr. condio—[3, 10], cōndĭtum—fr. condo—[3, 10], flētus [9], rāsit [7], dirŭtum [9], bĭberūnt [7, 3], hærēntis [2, 3], gāza [3.]

### EXAMPLES IN COMPOSITION.

Rule. *Implet et illa manum, sed parcius, ære minūto.* Juv.
  *Lumina rara micant, somno vinoque solūti.* Virg.
Exc. 1. *Exilium requiesque mihi, non fama petīta est.* Ov.
  *Ne male condĭtum jus apponatur; ut omnes.* Hor.
Exc. 2. *Discite justitiam monĭti, et non temnere Divos.*
  Virg.
Note. *Morte obĭta, quorum tellus amplectitur ossa.* Lucret.


### RULE XI.

### *Of Prepositions in Composition.*

Longa *a, de, e, se, di* præter *dĭrimo* atque *dĭsertus.*
Sit *Rĕ* breve, at *rēfert* a *res* producito semper.
Corripe *Pro* Græcum, sed produc rite Latinum.
Contrahe quæ *fundus, fugio, neptis*que *nepos*que,
Et *festus, fari, fateor, fanum*que crearunt.
Hisce *prŏfecto* addas, pariterque *prŏcella, prŏtervus;*
At primam variant *prŏpago, prŏpina, prŏfundo,*
*Prŏpulso, prŏcurro, prŏpello; Prŏserpina* junge.,
Corripe *ab,* et *reliquas,* obstet nisi consona bina.

In compound words, the prepositions or particles *a, de, e, se, di,* are long; as, āmitto, dēduco, ērumpo, sēparo, dīrigo.

Excep. 1. *Di* in *dĭrimo* and *dĭsertus,* is short.

Excep. 2. *Re* is generally short; as, *rĕlinquo, rĕfero*: but *re* in *rēfert*, the impersonal verb ["it concerns"] from the substantive *rēs*, has the first syllable long.

Excep. 3. *Pro* is short in Greek words; as, *Prŏmetheus, Prŏpontis*: in Latin words it is usually long; as, *prōcudo, prōcurvus, prōveho*: except when compounded with the words enumerated in the rule; as, *prŏfundus, prŏfugio, prŏneptis*, &c., &c.

Excep. 4. In the following words the *pro* is doubtful; viz., *prŏpago, prŏpino, prŏfundo*, &c., as given in the rule.

Excep. 5. The prepositions *ab, ad, in, ob, per,* and *sub,* are short in composition before vowels; as are also the final syllables of *ante, circum* and *super;* as, *ăbeo, ădero, circŭmago, supĕraddo,* &c., &c.

Note. *Trans* in composition frequently drops the last two letters, still preserving its proper quantity; as, *trādo* [from *transdo*]; *trāduco* [from *transduco*]. *Ob* and *ab* in like manner, before a consonant—where they should become long by position—drop the final letter, still retaining the short quantity; as, *ŏmitto* [from *ŏbmitto*], *ăperio*, [from *ābperio*].

### EXAMPLES BY SINGLE WORDS.

*Rule.* Āmisit, dēduxit, dīvisus. *Excep.* 1. Dĭrimo, dĭsertus. *Excep.* 2. Rĕtulit, rĕditus, rĕfert ("brings back") rēfert ("it concerns." *Excep.* 3. Prŏpontis, prŏpheta, prŏlogus: prōcessit, prōmisit: prŏfundus, prŏcella, prŏfectus, prŏficiscor. *Excep.* 4. Prŏpago, prŏpino prŏpulso. *Excep.* 5. Ăbesset, ădegit, ăbitus, circŭmagis; ădmitto, pērcello.

*Note.* Trāno, ŏmitto.

*Promiscuous Examples.* Quæsītum [2, 10], rĕdītum [11, 9], ējĭcĭunt [11, 6, 1], rătas [9], sūstŭlerŭnt [3, 7, 3], pĕrēgit [11, 7], vetĭtum [10], dĕōsculor [1, 3], dătus [9], aūdiit [2, 1].

### EXAMPLES IN COMPOSITION.

Rule. *Āmissos longo socios sermone requirunt.*    Virg.
Exc. 1. *Cede deo dixitque et prœlia voce dĭremit.*    Id.
     2. *Quid tamen hoc rēfert, si se pro classe Pelasga*
        *Arma tulisse rĕfert.*    .    .    .    Ovid.
   3. *Qualiter in Scythicâ religatus rupe Prŏmetheus.* Mart.
     *Prōvehimur portu ; terrœque urbesque recedunt.* Virg.
Exc. 4. *Sed truncis oleœ melius, prōpagine vites.*    Id.
   5. *Omnibus umbra locis ădero, dabis, improbe, pœnas.* Id.
Note. *Pleraque differat, et presens in tempus ŏmittat.* Hor.

### RULE XII.

*Of A, E, and I, in compound words.*

Produc *a* semper composti parte priori,
Ac simul *e*, simul *i*, ferme breviare memento ;
Nēquidquam produc, nēquando, venēfica, nēquam,
Nēquaquam, nēquis sociosque ; vidēlicet addas.
Īdem masculeum produc, et sīquis, ibīdem,
Scīlicet et bīgœ, tibīcen, ubīque, quadrīgœ,
Bīmus, tantīdem, quīdam et composta diei.
Compositum variabis ubĭ ; variabis ibĭdem.

A in the first part of a compound Latin word,* is long ; as *trādo, mālo, quāre, quātenus.* E in the first part of compounds, is generally short ; as, *liquĕfacio, ĕquidem,*

---

    * In Greek compounds, the *a* is sometimes long ; as, *Neāpolis ;* and sometimes short ; as, *ălipsos :* these words, however, belong to the rules of Greek Prosody.
    † In *Mālo*, the *a*—originally short in *măgis*—becomes long in the compound, by syncope and crasis; thus, *Mă'volo*, or *Măwolo, Maw'lo, Mālo.*

*nĕfas, trĕcenti;*\* in like manner, *i* in the first part of a compound, is generally short; as, *omnĭpotens, causĭdicus, bĭceps, sĭquidem.*

Excep. 1. *Nēquidquam, nēquando,* and the other words enumerated in the rule, with *nēquis, nēqua, nēquid,* have the *ē* long. *Sēmodius, sēmestris, sēdecim,* have the *e* long. *Sĕlibra* is short in Martial.

Excep. 2. *Idem* (mascul.), *sīquis, ibīdem, scīlicet, bīgæ,* and the other words enumerated, have the *i* long; as also, *bīduum, trīduum, quotīdie,* and other compounds of *dies. Ludīmagister, lucrīfacio, agrīcultura,* and a few others have the *i* long. *Tibīcen* has the second syllable long, being formed by crasis from *Tibiicen;* but *Tubĭcen* is short according to the rule. The first *i* in *nīmirum* is also long :—the second being long from derivation.

Note. The *a* in *eădem* is short, unless it should be the ablative case. Although in *ubīque* and *ibīdem* the middle syllable is long according to the rule, in *ubĭcunque* and *ubĭvis,* it is common; as in the primitive *ubĭ.*

### EXAMPLES BY SINGLE WORDS.

*On Rule.* Quāre, trāductum, quācunque; patĕfecit, nĕqueo, valĕdica; fatīdicus, signĭfico, tubĭcen.

*Excep.* 1. Nēquaquam, vidēlicet, sēcedo. *Excep.* 2. Scīlicet, tantīdem, merīdies, tibīcen.

*Promiscuous Examples.* Unĭgĕnĭtus [12, 5, 5], ăbēst [11, 3], gavisum [10], flēturi [9], tetĭgīsse [8, 8, 3], crēvi [7], venūmdăta [3, 6], repŭdĭum—fr. pŭdor—[5, 1], migrāntes [4, 3], rējice [3], cœlum [2], pătrĭæ [4, 1, 2].

### EXAMPLES IN COMPOSITION.

Rule. *Quāre agite ô proprios generatim discite cultus.* Vir.
*Sæpe petens Hero, juvenis trānavĕrat undas.* Ovid.

---

\* And all compounds from *tres* or *tris ;* as. *trĕdecim, trĭplex, trĭformis,* &c.; but the *i* in *trĭginta* and its derivatives *trĭgesimus, trĭceni,* &c., is long, because *trĭginta* is not, properly speaking, a compound word; *ginta* being merely a termination.

*Credebant hoc grande nĕfas, et morte piandum.* Juv.
*Dum nimium vano tumēfactus nomine gaudes.* Mart.
*Tum pater omnĭpotens, rerum cui summa potestas.* Vir.
Exc. 1. *Barbara narratus venisse venēfica tecum.* Ovid.
Exc. 2. *Omnibus idem animus, scelerata excedere terra.* Vir.
Note. *Canities eădem est, eădem violentia vultu.* Ovid.

### RULE XIII.

*Of the O, U, and Y, in Composition.*

Græcum *O-micron*, prima compôsti corripe parte;
*O-mega* produces: ast *Y-psilon* breviabis.—
O Latium in variis breviat vel protrahit usus.
U brevia, ut *Locŭples, Quadrŭplex:* sed *Jūpiter*, atque
*Jūdex, jūdicium*, primam producere gaudent.

Compound words of Greek origin and terminating the first member of the compound with the letter *o* (*omicron*), have that letter short; as, *bibliŏpola, Areŏpagus:*—unless where it becomes common or long from position; as, *chirŏgraphus, Philōxenus.* If the first member of the compound end with *o* (*omega*), the vowel is long in Latin; as, *Minōtaurus, geōgraphus.* When *y* terminates the first member of the compound, it is generally short; as, *Thrasȳbulus, polȳpus;* unless rendered common or long by position; as, *Polȳcletus, Polȳxena.* O in compound Latin words, is sometimes long and sometimes short; as, *quandōque, nōlo, quōque* (the ablative); *quandŏquidem, hŏdie, quŏque,* (the particle). U in similar situations, is generally short; as, *locŭples, trojŭgena;* but *Jūpiter, jūdex,* and *jūdicium,* have the *u* long.

### EXAMPLES BY SINGLE WORDS.

*Rule.* Argŏnauta, Arctŏphylax; Hippŏcrene, Nicŏstratus; geōmetres, lagōpus; aliŏquin, utrŏbique; Eurȳpylus, Polȳdamus; Polȳcletus, Polȳxena; quōcirca, quōminus;

sacrŏsanctus, duŏdecim; quadrŭpes, centŭplex; jūdicat, jūdex.

*Promiscuous Examples.* Rĕcŭbāns [11, 5, 3], Dĕus [1], fīet [1], glaciēi [1], fĕcit [7], illĭus [3, 1], ăgrēstis [4, 3], ĕquidem [12], ădĕo [11, 1], Thessalŏnīca [13, 6], prŏtenus [11], vĭx [3], prædīxit [2, 3], extŭlit [3, 7], nīmirum [12, 6], dīus [Gr. 1], fūsos [9], prŏcēlla [11, 3], Polȳdorus [13], locūtus [10], ĭnhŭmatus [11, 5], īdem *neut.* [12].

### EXAMPLES IN COMPOSITION.

Rule. *Hesperios auxit tantum Cleŏpatra furores.* Lucan.
*Nititur hinc Taläus, fratrisque Leōdocus urget.* Val. Flac.
*Nam qualis quantusque cavo Polȳphemus in antro.* Virg.
*Indignor quandōque bonus dormitat Homerus.* Hor.
*Tollit se arrectum quadrŭpes, et saucius auras.* Virg.

### ON THE INCREMENTS OF NOUNS.

A noun is said to increase or have an increment, when any of its oblique* cases has a syllable more than the nominative. If the genitive,—by whose increment that of all the other† oblique cases is regulated—has the same number of syllables as the nominative, then there is no increment; as, *musa, musæ; dominus, domini;* but if the number of syllables be greater, then there is an increment, which must be the penultima‡ of the case so increasing; as, *musarum—[mu-SA-rum], dominorum—[domi-NO-rum]*, where *SA* and *NO* are the increments.

When any case has a syllable more than such increasing genitive, it is said to have a second increment; as from *animal* comes *ani-MA-lis*, with one increment, and from *animalis* come *ani-MA-LI-a, ani-MA-LI-um, ani-*

---

* All cases except the nom. and voc. sing., are called oblique cases.
† Except the acc. sing. of neuters of fifth declension, and of some Greek nouns in *is ;* as *Paris*, &c.
‡ The last syllable is never regarded as an increment; thus, in words of one syllable, as *rex*, (*regis*,) *re*, the penultima of the gen. is the increment.

*MA-LI-bus* with two increments: *MA* being the first, and *LI* the second, increment. Whether the increment of the genitive sing. be long or short, it remains the same throughout all the oblique cases; as, *sermōnis, sermōni, sermōnibus*, &c., &c.; *Cæsăris, Cæsări, Cæsărum*, &c., &c.; except *bōbus* or *būbus*, which has a long increment, although the genitive is short.\* *Iter, jecur, supellex*, and compounds of *caput* are said to have double increments; as, *itineris, jecinoris, supellectilis, ancipitis;* but these genitives come in reality from obsolete nominatives, viz., *itiner, jecinur, supellectilis, ancipes*.

### RULE XIV.

*Increments of the first and second Declension.*

Casibus obliquis vix crescit prima. Secunda
Corripit incrementa; tamen producit *Ibēri*.

The first declension has no increment; except among the poets, in the resolution of *æ* into *aï*, as *aulāï, pictāï*, where the *a* is long. In the second declension, the increment is short; as *pŭeri, vĭri, satŭri*.†

Excep. *Iber* and its compound *Celtiber* have the penultima of the genitive long; as, *Ibēros, Celtibēri*.‡

EXAMPLES BY SINGLE WORDS.

*Rule.* Pictāï, aurāï; mĭseri, domĭni. *Excep.* Ibēri, Celtibēri.

*Promiscuous Examples.* Darīus [Gr. 1], præĭret [2], diffīdit [3, 7], sătum [9], dirŭtus [11, 9], credĭtus [10], prŏfŭndus [11, 3], dĕhīscat [1, 3], ōmnĭpŏtens [3, 12, 5— fr. pŏtens—wh. fr. pŏtis].

---

\* This however cannot be considered an exception, whereas it comes from *bŏvĭbus* or *bŏwĭbus*, by syncope *Bŏwbus*, and by crasis *bĕbus*.

† These cannot, strictly speaking, be regarded as increments, whereas they come from the old nominatives *puerus, virus, saturus*.

‡ These two words are in like manner without any real increment; for the genitive sin. and the nom. plural *Iberi* are both formed regularly from the nom. sin. *Iberus*. There is another from *Iber, Iberos*, or *Iberis*, which belongs to the 3d declension. Both forms are borrowed from the Greek:— Ἰβηρος, Ἰβηρου— Ἰβηρ, Ἰβηρος.

### EXAMPLES IN COMPOSITION.

Rule. *Æthereum sensum, atque auräi simplicis ignem.*
　　　　　　　　　　　　　　　　　　　　　　　　Virg.
　*O pŭeri! ne tanta animis assuescite bella.* 　Id.
Excep. *Quique feros movit Sertorius exul Ibēros.* Lucan.

### RULE XV.

*Increments of the third Declension in* **A**.

Nominis *a* crescens, quod flectit tertia, longum est.
　Mascula corripies *-al* et *-ar* finita, simulque
*Par* cum compositis, *hepar*, cum *nectăre, bacchar,*
Cum *văde, mas,* et *anas,* cui junge *lăremque jubar*que.

The increment of *a* in nouns of the third declension is generally long; as, *pax, pācis; pietas, pietātis; vectigal, vectigālis.*

Excep. Proper names of the masculine gender ending in *al* and *ar* (except *Car* and *Nar*), have short increments; as, Hannibal, Hannibălis; Cæsar, Cæsăris: so also have *par* [the adjective] and its compounds; *par* the substantive, the noun *sal,* and the other words enumerated.

#### EXAMPLES BY SINGLE WORDS.

*Rule.* Ajācis, ætātis, calcāris. *Excep.* Asdrubălis, Amilcăris; părem, hepătis, nectăre, anătis—fr. anăs, "a duck."

*Promiscuous Examples.* Lărem [15], săle [15], pŭeros [1, 14], Hănnibălis [3, 15], quadrigæ [12, 2], piĕtātem [1, 15], ubĭque [12], prŏnepos [11], sŏnĭpes [5—fr. sŏnus, 12], circūmdăta [3, 9].

#### EXAMPLES IN COMPOSITION.

Rule. *Jane, fac æternos pācem pācisque ministros.* Ovid.
Exc. *Hannibălem Fabio ducam spectante per urbem.* Silius.
　*Vela dabant læti et spumas sălis ære ruebant.* 　Virg.
　*Errantes hederas passim cum baccăre tellus.* 　Id.
　*Sulphureas posuit spiramina Nāris ad undas.* Ennius.

## RULE XVI.

*Increments from A and AS.*

A quoque et *as* Græcum, breve postulat incrementum.
-*s* quoque finitum cum consona ponitur ante,
Et *dropax, anthrax, Atrax,* cum *smilŭce, climax;*
Adde *Atŭcem, panăcem, colăcem, styrăcem*que, *făcem*que,
Atque *abăcem, corăcem, phylăcem* compostaque, et *harpax.*

Greek nouns ending in *a* and *as*, have short increments; as, *poëma, poëmătis; lampas, lampădis:* also nouns ending with *s* preceded by a consonant; as, *Arabs, Arăbis; trabs, trăbis;* besides the following words in *ax-ăcis;* as, *dropax, anthrax, Atrax,*[*] &c., &c., and the compounds of *phylax* and *corax*, with *harpax, harpăgis,* and the like.

### EXAMPLES BY SINGLE WORDS.

*Rule.* Stemmăta, lampăde, poëmăte; Arăbum, trăbe, dropăce, făce, panăcem; &c.

*Promiscuous Examples.* Vădibus [15], Pallădis [3, 16], Titānas [15], jŭbăris [5, 15], satŭros [14], Cymŏthoë [Gr. 13], trĕcēnti [12, 3], prōcŭrrit [11, 3], āgnītus [3, 6], mollītum [10].

### EXAMPLES IN COMPOSITION.

Rule. *Undique collucent præcinctæ lampădes auro.* Ovid.
*Nam modo thurilegos Arăbas, modo suspicis Indos.* Id.
*Non styrăce Idæo fragrantes uncta capillos.* Virg. Cir.

## RULE XVII.

*Increments in E.*

Nominis *e* crescens numero breviabis utroque:
Excipe *Iber* patriosque -*ēnis* (sed contrahito *Hymen*),

---

[*] *Syphax, Syphăcis* is said to be common; but erroneously, for the passage in Claudian should have *Annibălem.*

## INCREMENTS OF THE THIRD DECLENSION.

*Ver, mansues, locuples, hæres, merces*que, *quies*que,
Et *vervex, lex, rex,* et *plebs, seps,* insuper *halec,*
-*el* peregrinum, -*es,* -*er* Græcum, *æthēre* et *äëre* demptis.
His addas *Sēris, Byzēris*que, et *Recimēris.*

The increment *e* of the third declension is generally short in both singular and plural; as, *grex, grĕgis; pes, pĕdis; mulier, muliĕrum; teres, terĕtis,* &c.

Excep. *Iber, Ibēris,* and genitives in *enis* (except *hymĕnis)* have the penultima long; as, *ren, rēnis, siren, sirēnis,* &c., as also *ver, mansues, locuples,* and the others enumerated. Hebrew nouns in *el;* as, *Daniel, Daniēlis,* and Greek nouns, in *es* and *er;* (except *æthĕris* and *äëre* from *æther* and *äer:*) as, *lebes, lebētis; crater, cratēris,* with *Sēris, Byzēris, Recimēris*—genitives from *Ser, Byzer,* and *Recimer*—have the increment long.

☞ Some foreign names in *ec* have the increment long by this rule; as, *Melchesidec, Melchesidēcis.*

#### EXAMPLES BY SINGLE WORDS.

*Rule.* Opĕri, pulvĕris, gregĭbus.  *Excep.* Ibēris, Sirēnis, (hymĕnis); vēris, mansuētis; lebētis, trapētis, (æthĕris): Michaēlis, Sēris, Recimēris.

*Promiscuous Examples.* Mērcēdis [3, 17], abăcis [16], māres [15], Cēltĭbēri [3, 5, 14], terĕtis [5,—fr. tĕro—17], pācem [15], tĕpĕfēcit [5, 12, 7], rĕsides [11], hymĕnis [17].

#### EXAMPLES IN COMPOSITION.

Rule. *Incumbens terĕti, Damon sic cœpit, olivæ.*     Virg.
Exc. *Monstra maris Sirēnes erant, quæ voce canora.* Ovid.
    *Cratēras magnos statuunt, et vina coronant.*    Virg.
    *Velleraque ut foliis depectant tenuia Sēres.*    Id.

## RULE XVIII

*Increments in I and Y.*

*I* aut *y* crescens numero breviabis utroque;
Græca sed in patrio casu *-ĭnis* et *-ўnis* adoptant;
Et *lis, glis, Samnis, Dis, gryps, Nesis*que, *Quiris*que
Cum *vibīce* simul, longa incrementa reposcunt.

The increment of the third declension is usually short; as, *lapis, lapĭdis; stips, stĭpis; pollex, pollĭcis.*

EXCEP. Genitives in *inis* and *ynis* from words of Greek origin, have the penultima long; as, *delphin, delphīnis; Phorcyn, Phorcȳnis;* as also, *lis, lītis; glis, glīris,* and the other words enumerated.

### EXAMPLES BY SINGLE WORDS.

*Rule.* Tegmĭne, sanguĭnis, ilĭce. *Excep.* Salamīnis, delphīnis; lītis, vibīce.

*Promiscuous Examples.* Æthĕre [2, 17], chlamȳdis or ȳdos [18], lebētes [Gr. 17], rēgĭbus [17, 18], trăbĭbus [16, 18], ænĭgmătis [2, 4, 16], calcăre [15], mulĭĕres [1, 17], ōrdĭnis [3. 18], Quirītis [18].

### EXAMPLES IN COMPOSITION.

Rule. *Tityre, tu patulæ recubans sub tegmĭne fagi.* Virg.
Exc. *Orpheus in silvis, inter delphīnas Arion.* Id.
 *Tradite nostra viris, ignavi, signa, Quirītes.* Luc.

## RULE XIX.

*Increments from IX and YX.*

*Ix* atque *-ўx* produc. *Histrix* cum *fornĭce, varix;*
*Coxendix, chœnix*que, *Cilix, natrix*que, *calix*que;
*Phryx*que, *larix,* et *onyx, pix, nix*que, *salix*que, *filix*que,

Contrahe ; *mastĭchis* his et *Eryx, calȳcis*que, et *Japyx*,
Conjungas : *sandix, Bebryx* variare memento.

Nouns ending in *ix* or *yx* most commonly lengthen the penultima of the genitive ; as, *felix, felīcis, bombyx, bombȳcis*.

EXCEP. 1. *Histrix, fornix, varix,* and the other words enumerated have the increment short: as also *appendix,* and some proper names ; as, *Ambiorix, Vercingetorix,* &c.

EXCEP. 2. *Bebryx* and *sandix* have the increment common.

NOTE. *Mastix, mastīgis,* "a whip," has the increment long.

### EXAMPLES BY SINGLE WORDS.

*Rule.* Ultrīcem, cervīcem, radīcis. *Excep.* 1. Coxendĭcem, nĭvem, pĭce. *Excep.* 2. Bebrȳcis, sandĭcis.

*Promiscuous Examples.* Prōspĕros [3,14], ēxēmplārĭa [3,3,15,1], Cæsăris [2, 15], Ārcădes [Gr. 3, 15], Cerĕris [17], quĭētem [1, 17], māgnētis [Gr. 4, 17,] capītis [18], līte [18,], strĭgis [19].

### EXAMPLES IN COMPOSITION.

Rule. *Tollite jampridem victrīcia tollite signa.* Lucan.
  *Ecce coturnīces inter sua prælia vivunt.* Ovid.
Exc. 1. *Fecundi calĭces quem non fecēre disertum?* Hor.
Exc. 2. *Bebrȳcis et Scythici procul inclementia sacra.*
             Val. Flac.
  *Possessus Baccho sæva Bebrȳcis in aula.* Silius.
Note. *Nunc mastīgophoris, oleoque et gymnadis arte.*
             Prudent.

### RULE XX.

*Increments in O.*

O crescens numero producimus usque priore.
O parvum in Græcis brevia, producito magnum.

Ausonius genitivus -*ŏris*, quem neutra dedere,
Corripitur ; propria huic junges, ut *Nestor* et *Hector ;*
*Os, ōris*, mediosque gradus extende, sed *arbos*,
Πούς composta, *lepus, memor*, et *bos, compos* et *impos*,
Corripe *Cappadŏcem, Allobrŏgem*, cum *præcŏce* et *obs, ops:*
Verum produces *Cercops, hydrops*que, *Cyclops*que.

In words of Latin origin the increment in *o* of the third declension is, for the most part, long; as, *sol, sōlis ; vox, vōcis ; victor, victōris*, and other verbal nouns in *or ;* —in *lepor, lepōris ;*\* *ros, rōris*, &c., &c. ; *statio, statiōnis*, and other verbals in *io ;*—in *Cato, Catōnis*, and other Latin proper names in *o*.

EXCEP. 1. Nouns in *o* or *on* from the Greek ων, preserve the quantity of the Greek increment. If that increment be formed with *omicron*, it is short; as, *sindon, sindŏnis ; Agamemnon, Agamemnŏnis ;*—if formed with *omega*, it is long; as, *Simon*, [or *Simo*], *Simōnis ; Plato*, [or *Platon*], *Platōnis*, &c.

OBSERV. 1. *Sidon, Orion, Ægeon*, and *Britto* have the increment common; while *Saxo, Seno*, and most other gentile nouns—or the names of nations and people —increase short.

EXCEP. 2. Genitives in *oris*† from Latin nouns of the neuter gender, have a short increment; as, *marmor, marmŏris ; corpus, cŏrporis*, &c.,—with Greek proper names in *or ;* as, *Hector, Hectŏris ; Nestor, Nestŏris*, &c., and also Latin appellations ; as, *rhetor, rhetŏris*, &c.

EXCEP. 3. *Os, ōris*, and adjectives of the comp. degree, have long increments; as, *melior, meliōris ; major, majōris*, &c.

EXCEP. 4. *Arbos*, compounds of πούς [as *tripus, polypus,*

---

\* *Lepus—ŏris* "a hare," has the increment short.
† *Ador, adŏris* of the masculine gen. is common.

## INCREMENTS OF THE THIRD DECLENSION. 31

*Œdipus*], *lepus, memor,* and other words specified, increase short.

Excep. 5. *Cappadox, Allobrox, præcox,* and òther words having a consonant before *s* in the nominative; as, *scobs, inops, Cecrops, Dolops,* have the increments short. Observ. 2. *Cyclops, Cercops,* and *hydrops* have long increments.

### EXAMPLES BY SINGLE WORDS.

*Rule.* Sermōnis, timōris, flōris, ratiōnis, Cicerōnis.

*Excep.* 1. Ædon, ædŏnis, halcyon, halcyŏnis; Solon, Solōnis, agon, agōnis. *Observ.* 1. Oriŏnis, Saxŏna. *Excep.* 2. Memŏris, ebŏris; Castŏris, rhetŏris. *Excep.* 3. Ōris, pejōris. *Excep.* 4. Bŏvis, Melampŏdis [fr. Melampus]. *Excep.* 5. Cappadŏcis, inŏpis. *Observ.* 2. Cyclōpis, Cercōpis.

*Promiscuous Examples.* Sōlem [20], Āllōbrŏges [3, 4, 20], fōrnĭce [3, 19], hymĕne [17], plēbi [17], vērvēcem [3, 17], dōgmăta [3, 16], Sirēnis [Gr. 17], Solōna [Gr. 20], robŏra [20].

### EXAMPLES IN COMPOSITION.

Rule. *Regia sōlis erat sublimibus alta columnis.* Ovid.
    *Nec victōris heri tetegit captiva cubile.* Virg.
    *Ire vetat, cursusque vagus statiōne moratur.* Lucan.

Exc. 1. *Pulsant, et pictis bellantur Amazōnes armis.* Virg.
    *Credit, et excludit sanos Helicōne poëtas.* Hor.

Observ. 1. *Ægæōna suis immania terga lacertis.* Ovid.
    *Audiêrat duros laxantem Ægæŏna nexus.* Statius.

Exc. 2. *Gratior et pulchro veniens in corpōre virtus.* Virg.
Exc. 3. *Componens manibusque manus, atque ōribus ōra.* Id.
Exc. 4. *Propter aquæ rivum sub ramis arbŏris altæ.*
                                         Lucan.

Exc. 5. *Mancipiis locuples, eget æris Cappadŏcum rex.*
Hor.
Ob. 2. *Tela reponuntur manibus fabriçata Cyclōpum.* Ov.

### RULE XXI.

*U brevia incrementa feret.*—Genitivus in *-ūris,*
*-ūdis* et *ūtis* ab *-us* producitur; adjice *fur, frux,*
*Lux, Pollux;* brevia *intercus*que, *percus*que, *Ligus*que.

The increment in *u* of the third declension is generally short; as, *murmur, murmŭris; dux, dŭcis; turtur, turtŭris,* &c., &c.

Excep. 1. Genitives in *udis, uris,* and *utis,* from nominatives in *us,* have the penultima long; as, *palus, palūdis; tellus, tellūris; incus, incūdis; virtus, virtūtis,* &c.; with *fur, fūris; lux, lūcis; Pollux, Pollūcis;* and *frūgis* from the obsolete nominative *frux.*

Excep. 2. *Intercus, pecus,* and *Ligus* have short increments.

#### EXAMPLES BY SINGLE WORDS.

*Rule.* Crŭcis, furfŭre, conjŭgis. *Excep.* 1. Incŭde, fŭris, salūtem. *Excep.* 2. Intercŭtis, pecŭde, Ligŭris.

*Promiscuous Examples.* Vŭltŭris [3, 21], decŏris [20], salūtem [21], nŭces [21], nĭvis [17], vērtĭci [3, 18], calĭcem [19], Nēstŏra [3, 20], laquĕāre [1, 15], duŏdeni [13].

#### EXAMPLES IN COMPOSITION.

Rule. *Consŭle nos, dŭce nos, dŭce jam victore, caremus.*
Pedo.
*Aspice, ventosi ceciderunt murmŭris auræ.* Virg.
Exc. 1. *Vix e conspectu Siculæ tellūris in altum.* Id.
Exc. 2. *Quid domini faciant, audent cum talia fūres.* Id.

### INCREMENTS OF THE OTHER DECLENSIONS. 77

The other declensions, like the first declension, have, properly speaking, no increment, unless in the plural cases.

### INCREMENTS OF THE PLURAL.

When the genitive or dative case plural contains a syllable more than the nominative plural, the penultima of such genitive or dative, is called the plural increment; as, *sa* in *musarum,* *bo* in *amborum* and *ambobus,* *bi* in *nubium* and *nubibus,* *quo* in *quorum,* *qui* in *quibus,* *re* in *rerum* and *rebus,* &c.

#### RULE XXII.

*Plural Increments in A, E, I, O, U.*

Pluralis casus si crescit, protrahit *a, e,*
Atque *o;* corripies *i, u;* verum excipe *būbus.*

The plural increments in *a, e,* and *o,* are long; as, *quārum, rērum, hōrum, dominōrum;* the increments in *i* and *u* are short; as, *quĭbus, montĭbus; lacŭbus, verŭbus,* —except the *u* in *būbus.*

##### EXAMPLES BY SINGLE WORDS.

*Rule.* Sylvārum, rērum, puerōrum: lapidĭbus, artŭbus:—būbus.

*Promiscuous Examples.* Vīrōrum [14, 22], filiārum [1, 22], parĭĕtĭbus [1, 17, 22], Arăris [15], părĭbus [15, 22], vădĭbus [15, 22], epĭgrămmăte [4, 3, 16], Pāllădis [3, Gr. 16], grĕgĭbus [17, 22].

##### EXAMPLES IN COMPOSITION.

Rule. *Appia, longārum, teritur, regina, viārum.* Statius.
*Arreptaque manu, " Quid agis, dulcissime rērum?"*
Hor.
*At Capys, et quōrum melior sententia menti.* Virg.
*Vivite felices, quĭbus est fortuna peracta.* Id.
Exc. *Consimili ratione venit būbus quoque sæpe.* Lucret.

#### INCREMENTS OF VERBS.

A verb is said to increase, when any of its tenses has

a syllable more in its *termination*,\* than the second person singular of the present tense indicative active.† This additional syllable is the *first* increment—the penultima: the final syllable being never called the increment. When the increasing part has another syllable added to it in the course of formation, the part so formed is the *second* increment, and so of the rest. Thus from *amas*—the standard or regulator—comes *a*-*ma*-*vi*, with one increment; from *amavi* comes *a*-*ma*-*ve*-*ram*, with two increments; from *amaveram*, comes *a*-*ma*-*ve*-*ra*-*mus*, with three; and in like manner *au*-di-e-ba-mi-*ni* from its regular formation with four increments. Any verb not exhibiting in any of its tenses or persons, a greater number of syllables than the regulator, is said to have no increment; thus, *amat*, *amant*, *ama*, *amem*, having no more syllables than *amas*, have no increment.

### RULE XXIII.

*Of the Increments of Verbs in A.*

*A* crescens produc—*Do* incremento excipe primo.

In the increments of verbs of every conjugation, the vowel *a* is long; as, *amābam*, *stāres*, *properāmus*, *audiebāmini*, &c.

EXCEP. The first increment (*only*) of the verb *do* is short; as, *dămus*, *dăbam*, *dăre*: hence also the short increment in the compounds *circumdămus*, *circumdăbant*, *venumdăbis*, *venumdăre*, &c.

---

\* Without the words "in its termination," the expression would not be either sufficiently limited or perspicuous; because the student might otherwise be induced to rank reduplicating verbs among these increments, which would be erroneous; whereas the increment in reduplicating verbs takes place at the beginning, by a prefix or argument; as, *cu*curri, *te*tendi, *mo*mordi, &c.

† The second person singular indicative active is the rule or measure, by which the increment is regulated.

☞ For deponent verbs, we may either suppose an active voice whence to procure a standard or regulator to determine the increments; or they can be regulated by other verbs of the same conjugation having an active voice. Thus for the deponent verb *gradior*, we may either suppose a fictitious active *gradio*, *gradis*, or be guided by *rapior*, which has a real active.

## INCREMENT OF VERBS IN E.

Obser. The *second* increment of *do*, not being an exception, follows the general rule; as, *dăbāmus, dăbātis, dăbāmini,* &c.

#### EXAMPLES BY SINGLE WORDS.

*Rule.* Amāmus, laudābāmus, docuerāmus. *Excep.* Dămus, dăte, circumdămus. *Observ.* Dăbāmus, dăbāmini, dăbātur.

*Promiscuous Examples.* Chorĕa [Gr. 1], prŏnūntīānt [11, 3, 1, 3], ālterĭus [3, 1], labātur [23], pēctŏre [3, 20], prĭōrem [1, 20], cūjus [3], Cȳclōpas [4, 20], sānguine [3, 18], fatīdĭcum [12, 6], aūdĭtus [2, 10].

#### EXAMPLES IN COMPOSITION.

Rule. *Et cantāre pares, et respondere parāti.* Virg.
  *Pugnabant armis, quæ post fabricāverat usus.* Hor.
Exc. *Multa rogant utenda dări, dăta reddere nolunt.* Ov.
Ob. *Nam quod consilium, aut quæ jam fortuna dăbātur.* Virg.

### RULE XXIV.
### *Increments of Verbs in* E.

E quoque producunt verba increscentia. Verum
Prima *e* corripiunt ante *r* duo tempora ternæ;
Dic-*bĕris* atque-*bĕre,* at-*rēris* producito-*rēre.*
Sit brevis *e* quando-*ram, -rim, -ro,* adjuncta sequuntur.
Corripit interdum *stetĕrunt dedĕrunt*que poeta.

In the increments of verbs, *e* is long; as, *amēmus, amavissētis, docēbam, legēris* and *legēre* (both fut. pass.), *audiēmus,* &c.

Excep. 1. **E** is short in the first increment of the first two tenses (pres. and imperf.) of the third conjugation; and also in the future terminations *bĕris* and *bĕre;* as, *cognoscĕre, legĕre, legĕrem, legĕremus; celebrabĕris, celebrabĕre,* &c.

OBSER. 1. But in the *second* increment when the word terminates in *rēris* or *rēre*, the *e* is long; as, *diripererēris, loquerēris, prosequerēre*, &c.

OBSER. 2. *Vĕlim, vĕlis, vĕlit*, &c., have the *e* short.

EXCEP. 2. The vowel *e* is short before *ram, rim, ro* of every conjugation; as, *amavĕram, amavĕrim, amavĕro, fecĕram, fecĕrim, fecĕro*, &c. The persons formed from them, retain the same quantity; as, *amavĕris, amavĕrit, fecĕrimus, fecĕritis*, &c.

OBSER. 3. The foregoing exception however does not apply to those syncopated tenses which have lost the syllable *ve;* as, *flēram, flērim, flēro;* because in these contracted forms, the *e* retains the quantity of the original form: viz.—*flē(ve)ram, flē(ve)rim*, &c.

EXCEP. 3 The poets sometimes shorten *e* before *runt*, in the third pers. plur. of the perf. indic. active; as, *stetĕrunt, tulĕrunt*, &c., &c.

### EXAMPLES BY SINGLE WORDS.

*Rule.* Amēmus, docērēmus, legērētis. *Excep.* 1. Legēret, legēre; amabēris, docebēre. *Observ.* 1. Amarēris, docerēre, *Observ.* 2. Vĕlitis, vĕlint. *Excep.* 2. Amavĕrat, docuĕris, legĕro. *Observ.* 3 Flēro, flēris. *Excep.* 3. Dedĕrunt, terruĕrunt.

*Promiscuous Examples.* Amāvērāmus [23, 24, 23], dăbātis [7, 23], lēgētis [24], docēto [24], dătum [9], stetĕrunt [7, 24], tŭlĕrunt [7, 24], pĕpĕrat [8], pătrīzo [4, 3].

### EXAMPLES IN COMPOSITION.

Rule. *Sic equidem ducēbam animo, rēbarque futurum.* Virg.
Exc. 1. *Jam legēre, et qua sit poteris cognoscĕre virtus.* Id.
     *Semper honore meo, semper celebrabēre donis.* Id.
Ob. 1. *Jungebam Phrygios, cum tu raperēre, leones.* Clau.
Ob. 2. *Musa, vĕlim memores; et quo patre natus uterque.*
     Hor.

Exc. 2. *Fecĕrat exiguas, jam Sol altissimus umbras.* Ov.
Ob. 3. *Implērunt montes, flērunt Rhodopeïæ arces.* Virg.
Exc. 3. *Dî tibi divitias dedērunt artemque fruendi.* Hor.

### RULE XXV.
### *Increment of Verbs in I.*

Corripit *I* crescens verbum. Sed deme *velīmus,
Nolīmus, sīmus,* quæque hinc composta dabuntur;
-*ivi* præteritum, præsens quartæ -*īmus*, et -*ītis.*
-*ri* conjunctivum possunt variare poëtæ.

In the increment of verbs—whether first, second, third, or fourth increment—*i* is generally short; as, *linquĭmus, amabĭmus, docebĭmini, audiebamĭni,* &c., with *venĭmus, reperĭmus,* &c., of the perfect tense.

EXCEP. 1. The *i* is long in *velīmus, velītis; nolīmus, volītis, nolīto; sīmus, sītis,* &c., with their compounds, *possīmus, adsīmus, prosīmus,* &c.

EXCEP. 2. The penultima of the preterite in *ivi* of any conjugation, is long; as, *petīvi, audīvi,* &c.; and also the first increment of the fourth conjugation, when followed by a consonant; as, *audīmus, audīrem, audīrer,* &c., and *venīmus, comperīmus,* &c., of the present tense; with the contracted form of the imperfect *audībam,* and the obsolete *audībo;* also found in *ībam* and *ībo* from *eo;* and in *quībam* and *quībo* from *queo.*

EXCEP. 3. In the penultima of the first and second pers. plur. of the indicative fut. perf. [or second future] and the perfect of the subjunctive, the *i* is common in poetry: —but in prose, it is usually long.

#### EXAMPLES BY SINGLE WORDS.

Amavĭmus, vivĭmus, iterabĭtis. *Excep.* 1. Nōlīte, nolītote, sītis, possītis. *Excep.* 2. Petīvi, qæsīvi; audītis,

---

* When the *i* is followed immediately by a vowel, it is of course short [by the Rule *Vocalem breviant,* &c.—]; as, *audĭunt, audĭens,* &c.

audīri; reperīmus (pres.); audībam, ībo, quībam. *Excep.*
3. Dederĭtis, dixerĭtis, contigerĭtis.
*Promiscuous Examples.* Audīvĕrāmus [25, 24, 23], docuērŭnt [24, 3], dĕdĕrant [9, 24], dămus [23], inĭtus [9], solūtus [10], quæsītus 10], nĕfas [12], vidēlicet [12], ambītus [6, exĭtus [9,] intrŏduco [13], animālis [15].

### EXAMPLES IN COMPOSITION.

Rule. *Victuros agĭmus semper, nec vivĭmus unquam.* Manil.
 *Scindĭtur interea studia in contraria vulgus.* Virg.
Exc. 1. *Et documenta damus, qua sīmus origine nati.* Ov.
 2. *Cessi, et sublato montem genitore petīvi.*   Virg.
  *Alterius sermone meros audīret honores.*   Hor.
  *Tu ne cede malis, sed contra audentior īto.* Virg.
 3. *Egerĭmus, nosti; et nimium meminisse necesse est.* Id.
  *Accepisse simul vitam dederĭtis in unda.*   Ovid.

### RULE XXVI.

*Increment of Verbs in O and U.*

*O* incrementum produc; *u* corripe semper
*U* fit in extremo penultima longa futuro.

The increment of verbs in *o* is always long;—that in *u* is generally short; as, *facitōte, habetōte; sŭmus, possŭmus, quæsŭmus.*

EXCEP. In the penultima of the future participle in *rus*, the *u* is always long; as, *peritūrus, factūrus, amatūrus.*

NOTE. To the long increment of verbs in *o*, some Prosodians regard the irregular verb, *fŏrem, fŏre,* an exception.

### EXAMPLES BY SINGLE WORDS.

*Rule.* Itōte, petitōte; malŭmus, volŭmus. *Excep.* Ventūrus, arsūrus.

*Promiscuous Examples.* ☞ The most useful mode of exercising the pupil in the increments of verbs, is to examine him in all the terminations of the four conjugations;. beginning with *amāmus.*

## EXAMPLES IN COMPOSITION.

Rule. *Hoc tamen amborum verbis estōte rogati.* Ovid.
*Cumque loqui poterit, matrem facitōte salutet.* Id.
*Nos numerus sŭmus, et fruges consumere nati.* Hor.
*Qui dare certa feræ, dare vulnera possŭmus hosti.* Ov.
*Si patriæ volŭmus, si nobis vivere chari.* Hor.
Exc. *Si peritūrus abis, et nos rape in omnia tecum.* Virg.
Note. *Hinc fōre ductores revocato a sanguine Teucri.* Virg.

### OF FINAL SYLLABLES.

The quantity of final syllables is ascertained,—by position; as, *prudēns, precōx ;*—by containing a diphthong; as, *musæ, pennæ ;*—or by special rules, as follows :—

### RULE XXVII.
### *Of Final A.*

*A* finita dato longis. *Ită, posteă,* deme,
*Eiă, quiă* et casus omnes: sed protrahe sextum;
Cui Græcos, ex *-as* primæ, conjunge vocandi.

*A* final, in words not declined by cases, [that is, in verbs and particles] is long; as, *amā, memorā ;\* frustrā, prætereā, posteā, postillā, ergā, intrā, ā,* &c., with the numerals in *gintā ;* as, *sexagintā, trigintā, quadrāgintā,* &c.

Excep. 1. In *ită, quiă, eiă, posteă,*—[the *a* in *postea* being common ;†]—also *puta* the adverb; the names of letters; as, *alphă, betă ;* and *hallelujă.*

Excep. 2. In most words declined by cases, the final

---

\* *Amā, memorā,* &c., have the final *a* long, because formed by crasis from *amae, memorae,* &c.

\* Many eminent Prosodians however insist, that the *a* in *postea, antea,* &c,. is always long ;—and that the syllable *ea* is in the ablative case sing. fem. ;— the prepositions becoming adverbs and the ablatives by their own power expressing a relation to some other word in the sentence. They add moreover, that whenever the syllable appears to be short, it is either in the accusative governed by the preposition, or must be pronounced in two syllables by crasis. See *Classical Journal* for April, 1817, *in loco.*

*a* is short; as, *musă*, [the nom.] *templă, Tydeă, lampadă, regnă.*

OBSERV. It is also short in Greek vocatives in *ă*, from nominatives in *es*, (changed to *a* in the Doric or Æolic dialect); as, *Orestă, Atrĭdă, Ætă, Thyestă, Circă*, &c.

EXCEP. 3. In the ablative sing. of the first declension, and in Greek vocatives from nominatives in *as* ; as, *prorā* [abl.], *pennā* [abl.] ; *Æneā, Calchā, Pallā.*

### EXAMPLES BY SINGLE WORDS.

*Rule.* Pugnā, intereā, contrā, trigintā. *Excep.* 1. Eiă, quiă, ită, puta (for videlicet). *Excep.* 2. Nemoră, tristiă, meă, Hectoră. *Observ.* Orestă, Anchisă, Circă. *Excep.* 3. Prorā, domină, quā ; Æneā, Lycidā.

*Promiscuous Examples.* Dominōrum [22], dĭēbus [1, 22], ūltrā [3, 27], Pōllūcis [3, 21], tēllūres [3, 21], velōcĭbus [20, 22], īmmemŏres [3, 20], Palæmŏnis [2, Gr. 20], bŏves [20], felĭcĭbus [18, 22], Dēlphīnes [Gr. 3, 18], līles [18].

### EXAMPLES IN COMPOSITION.

Rule. *Musa, mihi causas memorā ; quo numine læso.* Virg.
    *'Jam tenet Italiam : tamen ultrā pergere tendit.* Juv.
Exc. 1. *Haud ită me experti Bitias et Pandarus ingens.*
    Virg.
    *Hoc discunt omnes ante Alphă et Betă puellæ.* Juv.
Exc. 2. *Anchoră de prora jacitur ; stant littore puppes.*
    Virg.
Obs. *Te tamen, o parvæ rector Polydectă Seriphi.* Ovid.
Exc. 3. *Prospiciens, summā placidum caput extulit undā.*
    Id.
    *Quid miserum, Æneā, laceras ? Jam parce sepulto.* Id.

### RULE XXVIII.
### *Of Final E.*

E brevia.—Primæ quintæque vocabula produc ;
Cetē, ohē, Tempē, *ferme*que, *fere*que, *fame*que.

## FINAL E. 41

Adde *docē* similemque modum; monosyllaba, præter
Encliticas et syllabicas: *benĕ*que et *malĕ* demptis,
Atque *infernĕ, supernĕ*, adverbia cuncta secundæ.

Final *e* is generally short; as, *patrĕ, natĕ, fugĕ, legerĕ, nempĕ, illĕ, quoquĕ, penĕ*.

EXCEP. 1. It is long in all cases of the first and fifth* declensions; as, *Æglē, Thisbē, Melpomenē; fidē, famē*, with *rē* and *diē* and their compounds *quarē, hodiē, pridiē*, &c., as well as in the contracted genitive and dative, *diē, fidē*.

EXCEP. 2. The final *e* is long in contracted words, transplanted from the Greek, whether singular; as, *Diomedē, Achillē*, or in the nominative and accusative neuters plural; as, *cetē, melē, pelagē, tempē*—all wanting the singular.

EXCEP. 3. *Ohē, fermē*, and *ferē*, have the *e* final long. *Ferĕ* is short in Ausonius.

EXCEP. 4. Verbs of the second conjugation have *e* final long in the second person singular imperative active; as, *docē, gaudē, salvē, valē*, &c.

OBSERV. 1. *Cavĕ, vidĕ*, and *respondĕ* are sometimes found short.

EXCEP. 5. Adverbs formed from adjectives in *us*—or of the second declension—have the final *e* long; as, *placidē, probē, latē;* together with all adverbs of the superlative degree; as, *maximē, minimē, doctissimē*.

OBSERV. 2. *Benĕ, malĕ, infernĕ*, and *supernĕ*, with *magĕ* and *impunĕ*, have the final *e* short. Adverbs coming from adjectives of the third declension, have the last syllable short, agreeably to the general rule; as, *sublimĕ, dulcĕ, difficilĕ*, &c.

EXCEP. 6. Monosyllables in *e;* as, *mē, tē sē*, and *nē*, (lest or not) are long.

OBSER. 3. The enclitic particles *quĕ, vĕ, nĕ*, (interroga-

---

* In cases of the 1st declension, because it is equivalent to the Greek η; in cases of the 5th, because it is a contracted syllable.

tive) and the syllabic adjuncts, *ptĕ, cĕ, tĕ, dĕ,* &c., found in *suaptĕ, nostraptĕ, tutĕ, quamdĕ,* &c., are short. These, however, might be ranged under the general rule;—never standing alone.

### EXAMPLES BY SINGLE WORDS.

*Rule.* Frangerĕ, utilĕ, mentĕ. *Excep.* 1. Alcmenē, diē, requiē, hodiē. *Excep.* 2. Pelagē, cacoethē, Tempē. *Excep.* 3. Fermē, ferē, ohē. *Excep.* 4. Docē, monē, vidē. *Obser.* 1. Cavĕ, vidĕ, valĕ. *Excep.* 5. Summē, valdē, (for validē), sanē. *Obser.* 2. Infernĕ, benĕ, malĕ; dulcĕ, suavĕ. *Excep.* 6. Mē, sē, tē. *Obser.* 3. Quĕ, vĕ, tutĕ, hoscĕ.

**Promiscuous Examples.** Nūmĭnĕ [5,—fr. nŭo. *obsol.* —" to nod, to approve,"—wh. fr. νεύω,—18, 28], amārĕ [23, 28], Hēctŏră [3, 20, 27], opĕrĕ [17, 28], vēctĭgālĕ [3, 15, 28], pŏemātă [1, 16, 27], făcĕ [16, 28], merĭdĭĕ [12, 1, 28], ĭnhĭbĕ [11, 6, 28], ĭndīgnĕ [3, 3, 28], præ- cĭpŭĕ [2, 1, 28], valĕ [28], cavĕ [28].

### EXAMPLES IN COMPOSITION.

Rule. *Incipĕ, parvĕ puer, risu cognoscerĕ matrem.* Virg.
*Antĕ mare et tellus, et quod tegit omnia cœlum.* Ov.
Exc. 1. *Tros Anchisiadē, facilis descensus Averni.* Virg.
*Non venias quarē tam longo tempore Romam.* Mart.
Exc. 2. *At pelagē multa, et late substrata videmus.* Lucret.
Exc. 3. *Mobilis et varia est fermē naturā malorum.* Juv.
Exc. 4. *Gaudē, quod spectant oculi te mille loquentem.* Hor.
Ob. 1. *Vadĕ, valē: cavĕ ne titubes, mandataq; frangas.* Id.
Exc. 5. *Excipe sollicitos placidē, mea dona, libellos.* Mart.
Ob. 2. *Nil benĕ cum facias, facias attamen omnia belle.* Id.
Ex. 6. *Mē me, adsum qui feci; in mē convertite ferrum.* Vir.
Ob. 3. *Arma virumquĕ cano, Trojæ qui primus ab oris.*\* Id.

---

\* This well-known verse at the opening of the Æneis, affords a striking exemplification of the absurdity involved in attempting to read Latin verse according to the rules of English accentuation. " Here," says one of the ablest advocates

## RULE XXIX.

### Of Final I and Y.

*I* produc.—Brevia *nisĭ* cum *quasĭ*, Græcaque cuncta:
Jure *mihĭ*, variare, *tibĭ*que, *sibĭ*que solemus,
Sed mage corripies *ibĭ*, *ubĭ*, dissyllabon et *cuĭ;*
Sicutĭ sed breviant cum *sicubĭ, necubĭ*, vates :
Adfuerit nisi Crasis, *y* semper corripiendum est.

The final *i* is generally long; as, *dominī, patrī, Mercurī, meī, amarī, audī, ī, Ovidī, filī.*\*

EXCEP. 1. The final vowel is usually short in *nisĭ* and *quasĭ*. In Greek words also, the final *i* and *y* are short; as, *sinapĭ*, *molў*—in vocatives of the third declen.; as, *Thetĭ, Parĭ, Daphnĭ, Tethў,* (uncontracted);—in the dat. sing. of Greek nouns; as, *Palladĭ, Thetidĭ;*—and in datives and ablatives plur.; as, *heroisĭ, Troasĭ, Dryasĭ.*

OBSERV. In *Tethȳ*, the contract. dative for *Tethyi*, the *y* is long.

EXCEP. 2. In *mihĭ, tibĭ, sibĭ,* and also in *ibĭ, ubĭ,* and *utĭ,* the final *i* is common. *Cuĭ* when a dissyllable has the *i* common.

EXCEP. 3. *Necubĭ, sicubĭ,* and *sicutī* are said to have the final vowel short :—but the *i* in the two former is common.

### EXAMPLES BY SINGLE WORDS.

*Rule.* Oculī, Mercurī, classī. *Fxcep.* 1. Nisī, quasī; gummī, melī; Tethȳ, Alexĭ; Paridĭ, Thetidĭ; Charisĭ,

---

of the modern system—"here, agreeably to the analogy of the English, every judicious reader will pronounce the syllables *vi* and *ca,* in the words *virum* and *cano,* long"! And such in reality is the fact!! Now let the Classical student observe the consequence of this "judicious" practice: by making these two syllables long, the two dactyles with which the line commences, are metamorphosed into as many Amphimacers; thus—*ārmă, virŭmqŭe, -cā!* and the line is made to contain 26 instead of 24 times!! while the sweetness, melody and rythmical connection are totally destroyed : a medley of versification never surely contemplated by the most elaborate and ornate of the Roman poets. But the innovators who would thus barbarously disfigure the beautiful remains of antiquity—

> Tradam protervis in mare Creticum
> Portare ventis.

\* By crasis from *Ovidie, filie.*

schemasĭ, ethesĭ. *Observ.* Tethȳ. *Excep.* 2. Mihĭ, tibĭ, sibĭ; ibĭ, ubĭ, utĭ: cuĭ. *Excep.* 3. Necubĭ, sicubĭ, sicutĭ.

*Promiscuous Examples.* Amarȳllĭ [3, Gr. 29], lapīdī [15, 29], tāntanĕ [3, 28], hoscĕ [28], fĭerī [1, 29], quī [29], rĕīquĕ [1, 29, 28], dīēī, [1, 1, 29], mājōrī [3, 20, 29], volŭcrī [4, 29], vēnī [7, 29], vīcīstī [7, 4, 29], tŭlīstī [7, 3, 29], tĕtĕndīstī [8, 3, 3, 29].

### EXAMPLES IN COMPOSITION.

Rule. *Quid dominī faciānt, audent cum talia fures.* Virg.
*Ī, sequere Italiam ventis, pete regna per undas.* Id.

Exc. 1. *Sic quasĭ Pythagoræ loqueris successor et hæres.*
Mart.
*Molȳ vocant superi: nigrâ radice tenetur.* Ovid.
*Semper Adonĭ, mei, repetitaque mortis imago.* Id.
*Palladĭ littoreæ celebrabat Scyros honorem.* Statius.
*Troasĭn\* invideo; quæ si lacrymosa suorum.* Ovid.

Exc. 2. *Tros Tyriusque mihī nullo discrimine agetur.* Vir.
*Non mihi si linguæ centum sint, oræque centum.* Id.

Exc. 3. *Sicubĭ magna Jovis antiquo robore quercus.* Id.

### RULE XXX.
## *Of Final O.*

*O* datur ambiguis.—Græca et monosyllaba longis.
*Ergō* pro causa, ternus sextusque secundæ,
Atque adverbia nomine, vel pronomine nata:
*Immŏ, modŏ,* et *citŏ* corripias; varia *postremŏ.*
*Serŏ, idcircŏ, ideŏ, verŏ, porrŏ*que *retrŏ*que.

*O* at the end of words is common;† as, *quandŏ, leŏ, duŏ, Catŏ, nolŏ.*

---
\* The *n* makes no difference in the quantity; being merely added to prevent the hiatus, arising from the concurrence of the two vowels: just as we say in English, "an orange," for "a orange,"—*euphoniæ gratia.*
† It is, however, more usually long than short.

Excep. 1. Greek cases written in the original with ω: as, *Androgeō, Cliō;* monosyllables; as, *ō, prō, dō; ergō,*\* signifying " for the sake of"—or, " on account of;" and datives and ablatives of the second declension; as, *somnō, tuō, ventō*—have the final vowel long.

Excep. 2. Adverbs derived from adjectives and pronouns have the final *ō* long; as, *subitō, meritō, multō, rarō, eō.*†

Observ. The final *o* is, however, short in *citŏ, immŏ, quomodŏ, dummodŏ, postmodŏ, modŏ,* (the adverb,) *egŏ,*‡ *octŏ.*

Excep. 3. The adverb *serŏ,* the conjunction *verŏ, postremŏ, idcircŏ,* and the other words enumerated, have the final *o* common.

### EXAMPLES BY SINGLE WORDS.

*Rule.* Quandŏ, præstŏ, Apollŏ, homŏ. *Excep.* 1. Athō, Alectō, prō, stō; deō, filiō. *Excep.* 2. Certō, tantō, falsō. *Observ.* 1. Quomodŏ, tantummodŏ, citŏ. *Excep.* 3. Idcircŏ, porrŏ, adeŏ, retrŏ.

*Promiscuous Examples.* Ērgō, [3, 30], Cliō [Gr. 1, 30], Cāntăbrō [3, 4, 30], mōtō [9, 30], dătă [9, 27], cōnsĭtī [3, 9, 29], solūtō [10, 30], tacītō [10, 28], sŭbĭtō [11, 9, 30], vigīntī [3, 29], Achīllē [3, 28], plorā [27], facĭtōtĕ [25, 26, 28], pĕcūnīæ [5, 5—fr. pĕcū, " cattle, sheep," anciently used in barter for money—1, 2].

### EXAMPLES IN COMPOSITION.

*Rule. Ambō florentes ætatibus, Arcades ambō.*    Virg.
*Ambō relucentes, ambō candore togati.*    Mant.
*Exc.* 1. *In foribus letum Androgeō; tum pendere pœnas.*
                                                                     Virg.

---

\* *Ergo,* signifying " therefore," is common, according to the general rule.
† These are commonly considered as ablatives of the second declension; but might they not be regarded as imitations of the Greek termination ως, with the *s* elided; agreeably to the Greek usage?
‡ Carey, however, makes the final vowel in *ego* common.

Ō patribus plebes, ō digni consule patres! Claud.
Aurō pulsa fides, aurō venalia jura. Propert.
Exc. 2. Pœna autem vehemens, et multō sævior illis. Juv.
Ibit eō, quo vis, qui zonam perdidit, inquit. Hor.
Obs. Ast egŏ quæ divum incedo regina, Jovisque. Virg.
Exc. 3. Imperium tibi serŏ datum; victoria velox. Claud.
Hic verō victus genitor se tollit ad auras. Virg.

### RULE XXXI.

*Final U long; B, T, D, short.*

*U* semper produc; *b, t, d*, corripe semper.
*B* produc peregrinum, at contrahe *nenŭ*que et *indŭ*.

The final *u* is generally long; as, *manū, cornū, metū, Panthū*, (Gr. voc.) *diū.* Latin words terminating in *b, t,* or *d*, usually have the final vowel short; as, *ăb, quĭd, ĕt, amăt.* ☞ Foreign words are commonly long; as, *Jōb, Jacōb; Davīd, Benadād.*

Excep. *Indŭ* and *menŭ* have the *u* short: as also have many words ending with short *ŭs;* by the elision of the final *s*, to prevent the vowel from becoming long by its position before the succeeding consonant; as, *plenŭ'*, for *plenŭs; nuncĭŭ'*, for *nuncĭŭs.*

Observ. Third persons singular of the perfect tense, contracting *ivĭt* or *ūt* into *it*, or *avĭt* into *at*,—have the final vowel long (by Rule II); as, *petīt* for *petŭt* or *petivĭt; obīt* for *obŭt* or *obivĭt; irritāt* for *irritavĭt.*

#### EXAMPLES BY SINGLE WORDS.

*Rule.* Vultū, cornū, Melampū, (Gr. voc.) ŏb, capŭt, audiĕt, quĭd. *Excep.* Nenŭ, indŭ ; plenŭ'. *Observ.* Abīt for abivĭt, petīt for petivĭt, creāt for creavĭt.

*Promiscuous Examples.* Amāvĕrĭt [23, 24, 31], pĕpĕrĭt [8, 8, 31], bĭbĭt [7, 31], fātĭdĭcō [5, 12, 6, 30], semĭsŏpītus

[12, 6, 10], prŏfŭgĭŏ [11, 6, 1, 30], ĭdem [neut. 12], quadrīgæ [12, 2], alīōquin [1, 13], indū [3, 31], gĕnĕrăt [5, 5, 31], ērŭmpĕrĕ [11, 3, 24, 28], rĕquīrŏ [11, 6—fr. quæro—30].

### EXAMPLES IN COMPOSITION.

Rule. *Parce metū Cytherea, manent immota tuorum.* Virg.
*Quo res summa loco, Panthū? quam prendimus arcem?* Id.

Exc. *Nec jacere indŭ manus, via qua munita fidei.* Lucret.
*Vicimus o socii, et magnam pugnavimŭ' pugnam.* En.

Obs. *Magnus civis obĭt, et formidatus Othoni.*  Juv.

### RULE XXXII.

### *Of Final C.*

C longum est. Brevia *nĕc, făc,* quibus adjice *donĕc.*
*Hĭc* pronomen, et *hŏc* primo et quarto variabis.

Final c has the preceding vowel generally long; as, *sīc, hūc, illīc, hīc,* (adv.), *hōc* (abl.)

Excep. 1. *Nĕc, donĕc,* and *făc* (imperative), have the final vowel short.

Excep. 2. The pronouns *hĭc* and *hŏc* (neut.), are common, but more frequently long than short. ☞ The imperatives *dīc* and *dūc* do not come under this rule, being only abbreviations of *dīce* and *dūce,* in which the quantity of *i* and *u* is not affected by the apocope of the final vowel.

### EXAMPLES BY SINGLE WORDS.

*Rule.* Sīc, hōc, illūc.  *Excep.* 1. Donĕc, nĕc, făc.
*Excep.* 2. Hĭc, hŏc.

*Promiscuous Examples.* Ită [27], Lycidā [Gr. voc. 27], famĕ [28], faciē [1, 28], rē [28], tacē [28], utī [29], Alēxī [2, Gr. 29], sibĭ [29], hūc [32], nĕc [31], prōnŭbă [11, 6, 27], lūdībrĭă [5, 4, 1, 27], cōntŭlĕrŏ [3, 7, 24, 30], cicătrīcis [4, 19].

### EXAMPLES IN COMPOSITION.

Rule. *Macte nova virtute, puer : sīc itur ad astra.* Virg.
Exc. 1. *Donĕc eris felix, multos numerabis amicos.* Ovid.
Exc. 2. *Hic gladio fidens, hīc acer et arduus hasta.* Virg.
*Hic vir hīc est, tibi quem promitti sæpius audis.* Id.

### RULE XXXIII.
### *Of Final L.*

Corripe *L.* At produc *sāl, sōl, nīl,* multaque Hebræa.

The final vowel before *l* is short; as, *mĕl, simŭl, nihĭl, consŭl, Asdrubăl.*

Excep. *Sāl, sōl,* and *nīl,* (contracted from *nihĭl,*) have the final vowel long; and also Hebrew names; as, *Daniēl, Raphaēl, Ismaēl.*

### EXAMPLES BY SINGLE WORDS.

*Rule.* Pŏl, fĕl, semĕl, famŭl. *Excep.* Sōl, sāl; Michaēl, Daniēl.

*Promiscuous Examples.* Nīl [33], nīhĭl [1, 33], hīc [adv. 32], vūltū [3, 31], nĕc [32], amŏ [30], măgīstrī [5—fr. măgis—3, 29], pœnĕ [2, 28], īnnīxă [3, 3, 27], facĭtōtĕ [25, 26, 28], aūdĭēbămĭnī [2, 1, 24, 23, 25, 29], lapĭdē [18, 29], līttŏrĭs [3, 20, 38], ōrĭs [from os, "a mouth," 20, 38].

### EXAMPLES IN COMPOSITION.

Rule. *Vertit terga citus damnatis, Asdrubăl ausis.* Silius.
*Obstupuit simŭl ipse, simŭl perculsus Achates.* Virg.
Exc. *De nihilo nihĭl, in nihilum nīl posse reverti.* Persius.
*Quum magnus Daniēl, qualis vir, quanta potestas!*
Tert.

☞ Respecting the quantity of final syllables in *m*, on which *P*rosodians are not agreed—it has been deemed advisable to insert no rule : as the subject may be more properly referred to the "Figures of *P*rosody;" farther on.

For the convenience, however, of teachers, who prefer the rule in the order of the letters, it is given below.*

RULE XXXIV.

### *Final N.*

*N* produc.—Breviabis at *-en* quod *-ĭnis* breve format;
Græcorum quartum, si sit brevis ultima recti;
*An, tamĕn, ĭn* cum compositis; rectumque secundæ.

Words, whether in Latin or of Greek origin, terminating with *n*, have the final vowel generally long; as, *ēn, splēn, quīn, sīn, Pān, Sirēn;* with *Actæōn, Lacedæmōn, Platōn,* &c., [written with an ω]; also Greek accusatives in *an* and *en,* of the first declen., from the nominatives in *as, es,* and *e* long; as, *Æneūn, Anchisēn, Calliopēn;* genitives plural; as, *Myrmidonōn, Cimmeriōn, epigrammatōn;* and Greek accusatives in *on* of the Attic dialect having ω in the original; as, *Athōn, Androgeōn.*

Excep. 1. Nouns terminating with *ĕn*, having *ĭnis* in the gen., have the final vowel short; as, *carmĕn, numĕn, nomĕn, tegmĕn, flumĕn.*

Excep. 2. The final vowel before *n*, is short in all Greek accusatives of every declension, whose nominative has a short final syllable; as, *Maiăn, Scorpiŏn.*

---

\* *M* vorat Ecthlipsis: prisci breviare solebant.
Final *m*, succeeded by a vowel [or the letter *h*.] is generally elided by Ecthlipsis: the older poets usually shortened the preceding vowel, preserving the *m* from elision: *ex. gr* :—
*Insignita, fere tum millia militŭm octo.* Ennius.

*Parĭn, Thetĭn, Itÿn, Alexĭn, chelÿn:* and datives plural in *in;* as, *Arcasĭn.*

Excep. 3. Ăn, tamĕn, ĭn, with their compounds, *forsăn, satĭn', veruntamēn,* &c., and *vidēn',* have the final vowel short.

Excep. 4. Greek nominatives in *on,* written with an *omicron,* and corresponding with the second declension in Latin, have the final syllable short; as, *Peliŏn, Iliŏn, Erotiŏn.*

Observ. Greek accusatives also in *ŏn* [omicron], have the final vowel short; as, *Cerberŏn, Rhodŏn, Menelaŏn.*

### EXAMPLES BY SINGLE WORDS.

*Rule.* Splēn, Titān, Sirēn, Salamīn, Cimmeriōn, Athōn.
*Excep.* 1. Pectĕn, flamĕn, crimĕn. *Excep.* 2. Ibīn, Æginān, Alexĭn. *Excep.* 3. Attamēn, vidĕn', satīn', nostīn'.
*Excep.* 4. Erotiŏn, Iliŏn, Peliŏn. *Observ.* Rhodŏn, Cerberŏn.

*Promiscuous Examples.* Tĭmĭdĭ [5,—fr. tĭmĕo—14, 29], ætātĕ [2, 15, 28], Cæsărĕ [2, 15, 28], exēmplārĭă [3, 3, 15, 1, 27], mulĭĕrĭbus [1, 17, 22], stēmmătă [3, 16, 27], rēnes [17], hymĕnæos [17, 2], mānsuēti [3, 17, 29], rēgĭbus [17, 22], rĕfĭcĭŏ [11, 6, 1, 30], ĭnĭquōrum [11, 6,—fr. æquus, 29].

### EXAMPLES IN COMPOSITION.

Rule. *De grege nōn ausim quicquam deponere tecum.* Virg.
*Finierat Titān; omnemque refugerat Orpheus.* Ov.
*Actæōn ego sum! dominum cognoscite vestrum.* Id.
*Amitto Anchisēn, hic me, pater optime, fessum.* Virg.
*Cimmeriōn etiam obscúras accessit ad oras.* Tibul.
Ex. 1. *Tegmĕn habent capiti; vestigia nuda sinistri.* Vir.
Ex. 2. *Namque ferunt raptam patriis Æginăn ab undis.* St.
Ex. 3. *Mittite;—forsăn et hæc olim meminisse juvabit.* Vir.

Ex. 4. *Ilĭŏn et Tenedos, Simoïsque et Xanthus et Ide.* Ov.
Obs. *Laudabunt alii claram Rhodōn, aut Mitylenen.* Hor.

### RULE XXXV.
### Final R.

*R* breve.—*Cūr* produc, *Fūr*, *Fār*, quibus adjice *Vēr*, *Nār;*
Et Graiûm quotquot longum dant *ēris* et *Æthēr*,
*Aēr*, *sēr*, et *Iber*.—Sit *Cŏr* breve.—*Celtibĕr* anceps.—
*Pār* cum compositis, et *lār*, producere vulgo
Norma jubet: sed tu monitus variabis utrumque.

Words ending in *r*, have the last vowel or syllable, for the most part, short; as, *Amilcăr, muliĕr; puĕr, tĕr, Hectŏr, martўr, sempĕr, precŏr, audientŭr*.

Excep. 1. *Cūr, fūr, fār, vēr,* and *nār,* have the final vowel long;—as also have all words of Greek origin, forming the genitive sing. in *ēris* long; as, *cratēr, statēr; aēr, æthēr, Sēr,* and *ibēr* :—but the compound of *ibēr* is common; as, *Celtibĕr,*

Obser. 1. *Patĕr* and *matĕr*, although increasing in the genitive, have the final vowel short, agreeably to the rule.

Obser. 2. *Cŏr* has the vowel short.

Excep. 2. *Păr* with its compounds, and *Lăr* have the final vowel generally common.\*

### EXAMPLES BY SINGLE WORDS.

*Rule.* Vĕr, timŏr, turtŭr, Hectŏr, amamŭr. *Excep.* 1. Cūr, vēr; statēr, spintēr, Recimēr; aēr, Sēr, ibēr :— Celtibĕr. *Observ.* Patĕr, matĕr. *Excep.* 2. Păr, Lăr.

---

\* Although the quantity of these two words is, in compliance with the authority of some excellent Prosodians, given as common, it must not be concealed, that many others of equal authority, agree with Alvary, in regarding it as always long.

*Promiscuous Examples.* Amărētŭr [23, 24, 35], æthĕrĕ, [2, 27, 28], tapētĭbus [17, 22], vīrgĭnĕ [3, 18, 28], Salamīnī [Gr. 18, 29], cōrnīcĕ [3, 19, 28], vĭgŏris [5,—fr. vīgeo, —20], æquŏră [2, 20, 27], dōctĭŏră [3, 1. 20, 27], mĕmŏrī [5,—fr. mĕmīni,—20, 29].

### EXAMPLES IN COMPOSITION.

Rule. *Sempĕr eris pauper, si paupĕr es, Æmiliane.* Mart.
 *Angustum formica terens itĕr, et bibit ingens.* Virg.
Exc. 1. *Multa quidem dixi, cūr excusatus abirem.*   Hor.
 *Inde mare, inde aēr, inde æthēr ignifer ipse.* Lucret.
Ob. 1. *Est mihi namque domi patĕr, est injusta noverca.*
              Virg.
Ob. 2. *Molle mihi levibusque cŏr est violable telis.*   Ovid.
Exc. 2. *Ludere pār impār, equitare in arundine longa.* Hor.

### RULE XXXVI.
### Final A S.

*Ās* produc.—Breve *Anăs.*—Græcorum tertia quartum.
Corripit—et rectum per *ădis* si patrius exit.

Words ending in *as* have the final vowel generally long; as, *crās, tempestās, Æneās, Pallās,* (*Pallantis*), *mūs, musās;*—all verbs terminating in *as;* such as, *amās, doceās, legebās;*—gentile nouns; as, *Arpinās, Antiās;*—and antique genitives; as, *viās, familiās.*

Excep. 1. *Anăs* is short.*

Excep. 2. Final *as* is also short in Greek accusatives plural of the third declension; as, *heroăs, lampadăs, delphinăs, Hectorăs, Heroidăs.*

Excep. 3. Greek nouns in *as,* forming the genitive in *ados* (*adis,* Latin), are short; as, *Arcăs,* (gen. *arcados* or *arcadis*); *Pallăs,* (gen. *Pallados* or *Palladis*): *lampăs,*

---

* In Petronius Arbiter. Burmann, however, conjectures the lection should be *avis.*

# FINAL ES.

*Iliăs* :—also Latin words in *as*, formed in the manner of Greek patronymics; as, *Appiăs, Adriăs, Honoriăs.*

### EXAMPLES BY SINGLE WORDS.

*Rule.* Fās, terrās, pietās, Æneās, Thomās, Pallās, (Pallantis), audiebās; Antiās, Larinās; curās, (gen.) tristitiās, (gen). *Excep.* 1. Anăs. *Excep.* 2. Cyclopăs, craterăs, Troăs, Naïdăs. *Excep.* 3. Lampăs, Pallăs, (Pallados), Iliăs; Appiăs, Adriăs.

*Promiscuous Examples.* Audīēbāmŭr [2, 1, 24, 23, 35], sōl [33], nēquis [12], nĕc [32], forsăn [34], omĕn [34], lōngē [3, 28 adv.], lāmpădās [3, 16, 26], scĭŏ [1, 30], Dīā [Gr. 1, 27], ēxtrā [3, 27], vivĭmus [25], Alēxāndrīā [Gr. 3, 3, 1, 27], mūsās [5,—fr. μᾶσα, "a muse,"—36].

### EXAMPLES IN COMPOSITION.

Rule. *Quid meus Æneās in te committere tantum?* Virg.
*Forte sua Libycis tempestās appulit oris.* Id.
Exc. 1. *Et pictis anăs enotata pennis.* (Phalœcian). Petro.
Exc. 2. *Orpheus in silvis, inter delphinăs Arion.* Virg.
Exc. 3. *Bellica Pallăs adest, et protegit ægide fratrem.* Ov.
*Adriăs unda vadis largam procul expuit algam.* Av.

### RULE XXXVII.

## Final ES.

*Es* dabitur longis.—Breviat sed tertia rectum,
Cum patrii brevis est crescens penultima; *pēs* hinc
Excipitur, *pariēs, ariēs, abiēs*que, *Cerēs*que.
Corripe et *ĕs* de *sum, penĕs,* et neutralia Græca.
His quintum et rectum numeri dent Græca secundi.

The final vowel in *es* is long; as, *rēs, quiēs, Alcidēs, sermonēs, docēs, essēs, deciēs;* with the nomin. and vocat. plur. of Greek nouns, (coming from the genitive sing. in *eos*), originally written with εις, contracted from εες; as, *hereses, crises, phrases.* The following also have *es* long: genitives of nouns in *e*, of the first declen., as, *Eurydicēs, Penelopēs, Idēs, Calliopēs;*—plural cases of Latin nouns of the third and fifth declensions, as, *Libyēs, Alphēs, rēs;* and the antique genitive in *es* of the fifth declension; as, *diēs, rabiēs.*

EXCEP. 1. Nouns in *es* of the third declension, increasing short in the genitive, have *es* in the nominative short: as, *hospĕs, alĕs, milĕs, præpĕs, limĕs.*

OBSERV. 1. *Ariēs, abiēs, pariēs, Cerēs* and *pēs,* with its compounds [*sonipēs, quadrupēs,* &c.,] are long, according to the rule.

EXCEP. 2. *Es* in the present tense of the verb *sum,* is short; as are also its compounds, *potĕs, abĕs, adĕs, prodĕs,* &c.; likewise the final *es* in the preposition, *penĕs;* and in Greek neuters, as, *cacoethĕs, hippomanĕs,* &c.; in Greek nominatives and vocatives plur. of nouns in the third declension, increasing in the genitive sing., but not forming that case in *eos;* as, *Tritonĕs, rhetorĕs, dæmonĕs, Arcadĕs, Troĕs:* and Greek vocatives sing., coming from nominatives in *es,* and forming the gen. in *eos;* as, *Demosthenĕs, Socratĕs,* &c.

OBSERV. 2. Wherever the Latin termination *es* represents the Greek termination ης, it is of course long; as, *Alcidēs, Brontēs, Palamedēs.*

### EXAMPLES BY SINGLE WORDS.

*Rule.* Nubēs, artēs, Joannēs, locuplēs, quotiēs, jubēs·, hæresēs, metamorphosēs; Calliopēs, Idēs, (both gen.); syrtēs, diēs; rabiēs, diēs, (both gen.): *Excep.* 1. Divĕs, pedĕs, segĕs. *Obser.* 1. Abiēs, pariēs, cornipēs. *Excep.* 2. Ĕs, potĕs, adĕs, penĕs; cacoethĕs, hippomanĕs; heroĕs, Amazonĕs, Troadĕs; Demosthenĕs, Socratĕs. *Obser.* 2. Brontēs, Palamedēs.

*Promiscuous Examples.* Pĕrītūrō [11, 9, 26, 30], Ārcădăs [3, Gr. 16, 36], arĭētēs [1, 17, 37], sēpĭbus [17, 22], Michäelis [17], velĭtis [*verb* 25], sūmus [26], nīsĭ [6,— fr. ně,—29], Pērsēs [3, 37], hăbītābās [5,—fr. hăbeo,—25, 23, 36], paūpěr [2, 35], Ænēān [2, Gr. 1, 34], ădēs [11, 37], fămă [5,—fr. φήμη,—27].

### EXAMPLES IN COMPOSITION.

Rule. *Orbus es, et locuplēs et Bruto consule dignus.* Mart.
*Anchisēs alacris palmas utrasque tetendit.* Virg.
*Alpēs ille quatit ; Rhodopeïa culmina lassat.* Claud.
Exc. 1. *Vivitur ex rapto : non hospēs ab hospite tutus.* Ov.
*Ætherea quos lapsa plagâ Jovis alēs aperto.* Virg.
Obs. 1. *Populus in fluviis, abiēs in montibus altis.* Id.
*Stat sonipēs et frœna ferox spumantia mandit.* Id.
Exc. 2. *Quisquis ěs, amissos hinc jam obliviscere Graios.* Id.
*Quem penēs arbitrium est, et jus et norma loquendi.*
Hor.
*Scribendi cacoëthēs, et ægro in corde senescit.* Juv.
*Ambo florentes ætatibus, Arcadēs ambo.* Virg.
Ob. 2. *Me ferus Alcidēs, tunc quum custode remoto.* Stat.

### RULE XXXVIII.

### *Final IS and YS.*

Corripies ĭs et y̆s.—Plurales excipe casus.
Glīs, sīs, vīs, verbum ac nomen, *nolīs*que, *velīs*que ;
Audīs, cum sociis ; quorum et genitivus in -*īnis*,
-*entis*ve, aut -*ītis* longum, producito semper.
rĭs conjunctivum mos est variare poëtis.

Final syllables in *is* and *ys*, have the vowel short ; as *apĭs, turrĭs, Jovĭs, militĭs, aspicĭs, creditĭs, bĭs, ĭs,* and *quĭs*, (nominatives), *Ity̆s, Capy̆s, Typhy̆s.*
Excep. 1. All plural cases ending in *is* have the final vowel long ; as, *musīs, virīs, armīs, vobīs, illīs, amarīs,* (adject.), *quīs* or *queīs* for *quibus, omnīs* for *omnes,* and

*urbĭs* for *urbes*. Contracted plurals, as *Erinnȳs* for *Erinnyes* or *Erinnyas* havs *ys* long.

Observ. 1. The adverbs *forīs*, *gratīs*, and *ingratīs*, have the final syllable long.*

Excep. 2. *Glīs*, *sīs*, (with its compounds†), *vīs*—whether verb or noun—*nolīs*, *velīs*, (with its compounds), *audīs*, and every second person singular of the fourth conjugation; as, *nescīs*, *sentīs*, &c., have the final vowel long.

Excep. 3. The final *is* is long in all nouns forming their genitive in *entis*, *inis*, or *itis*, with the penultima long; as, *Simoīs*, (*Simoēntis*), *Salamīs*, (*Salamīnis*), *līs*, (*lītis*).

Observ. 2. The termination *ris* in the second future indicative and perfect subjunctive, has the *i* common; as, *amaverĭs*, *dixerĭs*, *miscuerĭs*.

### EXAMPLES BY SINGLE WORDS.

*Rule.* Lapĭs, dulcĭs, aĭs, inquĭs, magĭs, cĭs, chelȳs, Erinnȳs. *Excep.* 1. Puerīs, glebīs, siccīs, quīs or queīs for quibus. *Observ.* 1. Forīs, gratīs. *Excep.* 2. Glīs, fīs, nescīs, vīs, quamvīs, sīs, adsīs. *Excep.* 3. Līs, dīs, Pyroīs, Quirīs. *Observ.* 2. Vitaverĭs, egerĭs, attulerĭs.

*Promiscuous Examples.* Prŏfŭndēns [11, 3, 3], prōcūrāvĭt [11, 5—fr. cūra—23, 31], nēquam [12], ŭbīquĕ [12, 28], hŏdĭē [13, 1, 28], ætātĭs [2, 15, 38], Amīlcărī [3, 15, 29], lămpădĭs [3, 16, 38], quămvīs [3, 38], Othrȳs [38], tŭlĕrĭs [7, 24, 38], stĕtĕrūnt [7, 24, 3], ĭmbĕr [3, 35].

### EXAMPLES IN COMPOSITION.

*Rule. Dulcĭs inexpertis cultura potentis amici.*     Hor.
       *Non apĭs inde tulit collectos sedula flores.*     Ovid.

---

\* These adverbs are in reality, datives or ablatives plural.
† Such as; *adsis, possis, malis, nolis quamvis*, &c.

FINAL OS. 57

*Donec eris felix, multos numerabĭs amicos.* Id.
*Atque utinam ex vobīs unus, vestrique fuissem.* Virg.
*At Capўs, et quorum melior sententia menti.* Id.
Exc. 1. *Præsentemque virīs intentant omnia mortem.* Id.
*Nobīs hæc portenta Deûm dedit ipse creator.* Cic.
Ob. 1. *Effugere haud potis est, ingratīs hæret et angit.* Luc.
Exc. 2. *Si vīs esse aliquis.—Probitas laudatur et alget.* Juv.
*Nescīs heu! nescis dominæ fastidia Romæ.* Mart.
Exc. 3. *Samnīs in ludo ac rudibus causis satis asper.* Lucil.
Obs. 2. *Græculus esuriens in cœlum, jusserĭs, ibit.* Juv.
*Miscuerīs elixa, simul conchylia turdis.* Hor.

RULE XXXIX.

*OS Final.*

Vult *os* produci.—*Compŏs* breviatur, et *impŏs*,
*Osque ossis :*—Graiûm neutralia jungito, ut *Argŏs*—
Et quot in *os* Latiæ flectuntur more secundæ,
Scripta per *o* parvum :—patrios, quibus adde Pelasgos.

Words terminating in *os* have the final vowel long; as, *flōs, nepōs, virōs, bonōs, vōs, ōs,* (*oris*), *Trōs, Minōs, Athōs,* and all other words which, in Greek, are written with ω; as, *Androgeōs;* with all proper names which change *laŏs* to *lĕōs* [Attically;] as, *Penelĕōs, Demolĕōs, Menelĕōs.*

EXCEP. 1. The final *os* is short in *compŏs, impŏs,* and *ŏs,* (*ossis*), with its compound *exŏs;* and in Greek neuters; as, *Argŏs, Chaŏs, melŏs.*

EXCEP. 2. All Greek nouns of the second declension—which in Greek are written with an *omicron*—have the final vowel short; as, *Tyrŏs, Arctŏs, Iliŏs.*

EXCEP. 3. All genitives in *os,* whatever be the nominative, are short; as, *Pallados, Oïleŏs, Orpheŏs, Tethyŏs.*

### EXAMPLES BY SINGLE WORDS.

*Rule.* Custōs, ventōs, jactatōs, nōs; Erectōs, herōs, Androgeōs, Nicoleōs. *Excep.* 1. Compŏs, impŏs, ŏs (ossis); chaŏs, epŏs. *Excep.* 2. Clarŏs, Tenedŏs, Atropŏs. *Excep.* 3. Arcadŏs, Tereŏs, Tethyŏs.

*Promiscuous Examples.* Honōs [39], vĭrōs [14, 39], mulĭĕrīs [1, 17, 38], lichēnēs [Gr. 17, 37], Ibērīs [17, 38], lēgī [dat. fr. lex, 17, 19], cĭtă [fr. cieo, 9, 27], dābĭtŭr [23, 25, 35], līttŏrīs [3, 20, 38], Ārgōnāutās [3, 13, 2, 36,] mē [28], cērvīcĭbus [3, 19, 22], dōnīs [5,—fr. δῶρον, "a gift," the ρ being changed into *n*,—38].

### EXAMPLES IN COMPOSITION.

Rule. *Ut flōs in septis secretus nascitur hortis.*   Catullus.
*Ōs homini sublime dedit, cœlumque tueri.*   Ovid.
*Androgeōs offert nobis, socia agmina credens.*   Virg.

Ex. 1. *Exŏs et exsanguis tumidos perfluctuat artus.* Lucret.
*Et Chaŏs, et Phlegethon, loca nocte silentia late.* Vir.

Ex. 2. *Et Tyrŏs instabilis, pretiosaque murice Sidon.* Luc.
Ex. 3. *O furor! o homines! dirique Prometheŏs artes!*
   Stat.

### RULE XL.

### *Final US.*

*Us* breve ponatur.—Produc monosyllaba, quæque
Casibus increscunt longis, et nomina quartæ,
(Exceptis recto et quinto), et quibus exit in *-untis,*
Patrias, et conflata a πούς, contractaque Græca
In recto ac patrio, et venerandum nomen IESUS.

Final *us* is short; as, *annŭs, cultŭs, tempŭs, fontibŭs, bonŭs, malŭs, illiŭs, dicimŭs, intŭs, tenŭs;* and also in the nominative and vocative sing. of the fourth declension; as, *domŭs, manŭs.*

## FINAL US.

EXCEP. 1. In monosyllables the *u* is long; as, *grūs, jūs, rūs, plūs.*

EXCEP. 2. All nouns having a long penultima in the genitive singular, are long in the nominative singular; as, *salūs, tellūs, palūs, virtūs.*

EXCEP. 3. All nouns of the fourth declension (the nominative and vocative singular excepted), have final *us* long; as, *aditūs, vultūs, fructūs.*

EXCEP. 4. In words from the Greek, forming their genitive in *untis*, as, *Opūs, Amathūs, Pessinūs*, the final *u* is long.

EXCEP. 5. Compounds from πούς, forming the genitive in *podis* or *podos*, as, *Tripūs, Melampūs, Œdipūs*, have the final *u* long.

OBSERV. *Polypŭs*, of the second declension, from the Doric, has the *u* short; as also have *Melampŭs* and *Œdipŭs* in like circumstances.

EXCEP. 6. In *Panthūs*, and other proper names, written in Greek, with the diphthong ους, contracted from οος, the final *u* is long;—and in genitives from nominatives fem. in *o* (ω); as, *Mantūs*, from nom. *Manto*; *Cliūs*, from nom. *Clio*; *Didūs*, nom. *Dido*, &c., &c.

EXCEP. 7. The final *u* is long in the venerable name of JESŪS.

### EXAMPLES BY SINGLE WORDS.

*Rule.* Opŭs, meliŭs, quibŭs, decimŭs, penitŭs; gradŭs, quæstŭs.

*Excep.* 1. Sūs, plūs, thūs. *Excep.* 2. Tellūs, salūs, palūs. *Excep.* 3. Fructūs, domūs, manūs. *Excep.* 4. Opūs, Amathūs, Pessinūs. *Excep.* 5. Tripūs, Polypūs, Œdipūs. *Observ.* Melampŭs, Polypŭs, (Doric 2d declens.) *Excep.* 6. Panthūs; Eratūs, Inūs, Clothūs. *Excep.* 7. Jesūs.

## FINAL US.

*Promiscuous Examples.* Tēllūs, (gen. tēllūris) [3, 40], sēnsĭbŭs [3, 22, 40], Pān [34], tŭlistī [7, 3, 29], dēdē̆runt [7, 24, 3], nēquă (fem. of nēquis,) [12, 27], prŏfēstŭs [11, 3, 40,] jūdēx [13, 3], ērūmpērĕ [11, 3, 24, 28], ăttĭgīt [3, 6, 31], mŏnĭmēntīs [5, 5, 3, 38], mŏvēndŭs [5,—fr. mŏveo,—3, 40], mōvīssēs [5,—fr. mōvi,—3, 37], mĕdĭŏcrīs [5,—fr. mĕdius,—1, 4, 38], frīgŏrībŭs [5,—fr. ῥῖγος, " cold," with the Æolic digamma (F) prefixed ; as, Fῥῖγος,—20, 22, 40].

### EXAMPLES IN COMPOSITION.

Rule. *Heu! fuge crudeles terras; fuge littŭs avarum*, Vir.
  *Seriŭs aut citius sedem properamŭs ad unam.* Ovid.
  *O patria! o divûm domŭs Ilium, et inclyta bello.* Vir.

Exc. 1. *Sed rigidum jūs est et inevitable mortis.*   Pedo.

Exc. 2. *Mox etiam fruges tellūs inarata ferebat.*   Ovid.
  *Regis opus; sterilisve palūs\* diŭ, aptaque remis.* Hor.

---

\* The author avails himself of the opportunity afforded by the introduction of this line from the "Art of Poetry," to make a few observations on the position of *palus*, so long a bone of contention among Prosodians ancient and modern. In most of the editions of Horace, the line is arranged thus:—
  Regis opus, sterilisque diu *palŭs*, aptaque remis:—
making the final syllable of *palus* short, contrary to Exception 2nd. of the above Rule. From the days of the commentator Servius, and the grammarian Priscian, down to the last elaborate edition of Horace by Professor Anthon, this line has been *crux grammaticorum*.
  The great Bentley would read—*palus prius.*—This emendation would indeed remedy the quantity, but at the expense of terseness and beauty. Carey supposes, that Horace might have intended *palus* to be of the 2nd or 4th declension, and thence make the final syllable short without any violation of quantity: while the learned professor of Columbia College contents himself with giving the various lections of preceding commentators without offering any thing new of his own. But, in truth, most of the conjectures, hitherto hazarded on the matter, are ingenious rather than satisfactory: for the only solution to the difficulty is that afforded by the arrangement given in our text;—which not only preserves the quantity, but detracts nothing from the harmony or rythmical beauty of the poet. The hepthemimeral cæsura too occurring at *lus of palus*, contributes at once to the strength as well as to the sweetness of the verse. Bentley's emendation does not, to be sure, alter the position of the cæsura, but the manifest inelegance of the *us* in *prius*, immediately succeeding the *us* in *palus*, is abhorrent to the *curiosa felicitas* of the great Lyric poet of antiquity.
  The quantity of the *u* in *diu*, which is long by nature, can oppose no serious objection to the arrangement adopted; as the instances among the classic authors

Ex. 3. *Quale manūs addunt ebori decus, aut ubi flavo.* Virg.
Ex. 4. *Est Amathūs, est celsa mihi Paphos, atque Cythera.*
*Id.*
Ex. 5. *Nil validæ juvêre manus, genitorque Melampūs.* Id.
Ob. *Utque sub æquoribus deprehensum polypŭs hostem.* Ovid.
Ex. 6. *Panthūs Othryades, arcis Phœbique sacerdos.* Virg.
Ex. 7. *Et cælo et terris venerandum nomen IESŪS.* Anon.

☞ OBSERVATION, on the *Final Syllable of a Verse*, as usually given on works on Prosody : thus—

*Syllaba cujuvis erit ultima carminis anceps.*

The final syllable of every verse, except the Anapæstic and the Ionic *a minore,*\* may be either long or short at the option of the poet ; or in the language of Prosodians, may be considered common ; *i. e.*, although the final syllable be naturally short, it may be reckoned long, and although naturally long, it may be reckoned short ; as—

*Gens inimica mihi Tyrrhenum navigat æquōr,*

where the final syllable ŏr, which is short by RULE XXXV, forms the second syllable of a spondee, to suit the purpose of the poet, and thus becomes long. Again in the following Sapphic from Horace—

*Crescit occulto velut arbor ævŏ,*

are numberless, where the long vowel or diphthong is made short, before another vowel or diphthong, by synalœpha or elision ; the diphthong or long vowel merely parting with one of its short component vowels, and remaining short : as—
    *Insulæ* Ionio in magno quas dira Celæno :—
where the *e* of the diphthong is elided :—and again,
    Ter sunt conati imponere *Peliŏ* Ossam :—
where the long vowel *o* in *Pelio* loses one of its two component short times, (or vowels,) and remains short before the succeeding vowel.

\* In both these species, the final syllable of the line or verse, if not naturally long, should, through means of the synapheia, be rendered long by the concourse of consonants.

the final syllable *vŏ*, which is in reality long, by RULE xxx., is used by the poet as if short, forming the second syllable of a trochee, to conclude his verse.

Such is the mode generally adopted by *P*rosodians to explain the final syllable of a verse. The truth however is, that the final syllable of every verse must be regarded as always long; (*necessario longa est ;*)—being either long by nature, or rendered so by the pause required at the end of every line: agreeably to the remarks of the judicious and elegant Clarke in his Notes on Homer:— Ultima cujusque versus syllaba, qualiscunque ea est natura....non (ut Grammatici loquuntur) communis, sed semper necessario longa est; propter pausam istam, quâ, fine versûs, syllabæ ultimæ pronunciatio necessario producitur.—*Ad Iliad*, A. 51.\*

### ON THE QUANTITY OF PENULTIMATE SYLLABLES NOT REDUCIBLE TO RULE.

1. *P*atronymics in *ides* or *ades*, have their penultimate generally short; as, *Priamĭdes, Atlantiădes*, &c., except those derived from nouns ending *eus ;* as, *Pelīdes, Tydīdes*, &c.; as—

Atque hic *Priamĭdem* laniatum corpore toto. *Virg.*
Par sibi *Pelīdes?* nec inania Tartara sentit. *Ovid.*

2. *P*atronymics and all kindred words in *äis, ëis, itis, öis, otis, ine*, and *one*, commonly lengthen the penultimate; as, *Achāis, Ptolemāis, Chrysēis, Ænēis, Memphītis, Oceanītis, Minōis, Latōis, Icariōtis, Nilōtis, Nerīne, Acrisiōne*. But *Thebăis* and *Phocăis* shorten the penultimate. *Nerĕis* is common.

Protinus Ægides, rapta *Minōide*, Dian. *Ovid.*
*Thebaĭdis* jussis sua tempora frondibus ornant. *Id.*

\* See also Cicero (Orator 64) and Quintilian (9, 4).

3. Adjectives in *acus, icus, idus,* and *imus,* usually shorten the penultimate; as, *Ægyptiăcus. dæmoniăcus; academĭcus, aromatĭcus; callĭdus, perfĭdus, lepĭdus; finitĭmus, legitĭmus;* also superlatives, *pulcherrĭmus, fortissĭmus, optĭmus, maxĭmus,* &c. Except *merācus, opācus; amīcus, aprīcus, pudīcus, mendīcus, postīcus; fīdus, infīdus; bīmus, trīmus; quadrīmus, patrīmus, matrīmus, opīmus;* and the two superlatives, *īmus* and *prīmus.*

Utque suum laqueis, quos *callĭdus* abdidit auceps. *Ov.*
———————— *Fidum* Æneas affatur Achaten. *Virg.*

4. Adjectives in *alis, anus, arus, irus, ivus, orus, osus, udus, urus,* and *utus,* have their penultimate long; as, *conjugālis, dotālis, urbānus, avārus, delīrus, æstīvus, fugitīvus, decōrus, formōsus, percrūdus, edūrus, astūtus.* But the penultimate of *barbărus, opipărus,* and *ovipărus,* are short.

Adjecisset opes, animi irritamen *avāri.* *Ovid.*
Pictus acu tunicas, et *barbăra* tegmina crurum. *Virg.*

5. Verbal adjectives in *ilis* shorten the penultimate; as, *agĭlis, facĭlis, fusĭlis, utĭlis,* &c. But adjectives derived from nouns are generally long; as, *anīlis, civīlis, herīlis,* &c., to which may be added *exīlis,* and *subtīlis;* also the names of months, *Aprīlis, Quinctīlis, Sextīlis:*—except *humĭlis, parĭlis,* and *simĭlis,* a word of uncertain origin, whose penultimates are short. But all adjectives in *atĭlis,* whether derived from verbs or nouns, have the penultimate short; as, *plicatĭlis, versatĭlis, volatĭlis, fluviatĭlis,* &c.

Nec tibi deliciæ *facĭles,* vulgataque tantum. *Ovid.*
At qui umbrata gerunt *civīli* tempora quercu. *Virg.*

6. Adjectives in *inus,* derived from living things, and denoting possession; also numeral distributives, proper names, and gentile nouns, lengthen the penultimate; as,

*Agnīnus, canīnus, leporīnus; Bīnus, trīnus, quīnus; Albīnus, Cratīnus, Justīnus; Alexandrīnus, Latīnus, Venusīnus,*[1] &c. To these may be added certain adjectives having a reference to physical or mental objects and designations; as, *adulterīnus, festīnus, gelasīnus, genuīnus, libertīnus, mediastīnus, opīnus,* and *inopīnus, paupertīnus, peregrīnus, supīnus.* Also, adjectives of place; as, *collīnus, marīnus, vicīnus;* and those derived from nouns denoting time; as, *matutīnus, vespertīnus;* and lastly these few, not reducible to a class, *Austrīnus, Caurīnus, cisternīnus, clandestīnus, repentīnus.*

> Sicaniam *peregrīna* colo . . . . .    *Ovid.*
> Et *matutīni* volucrum sub culmine cantus.   *Virg.*

7. Adjectives in *inus*, derived from inanimate things, such as plants, trees, stones, &c.; also from adverbs of time, or from substantives denoting the four seasons of the year, have their penultimate short; as, *Amaracĭnus, crocĭnus, hyacinthĭnus; cedrĭnus, fagĭnus, oleagĭnus; adamantĭnus, amethystĭnus, smaragdĭnus; corallĭnus, crystallĭnus, murrhĭnus; Crastĭnus, diutĭnus, perendĭnus, pristĭnus, serotĭnus; Earĭnus, oporĭnus, chimerĭnus, therĭnus;* also *annotĭnus, hornotĭnus.* To which add *bombycĭnus, elephantĭnus,* which seem to refer rather to the silk and ivory, than to the animals themselves.

> Et lux cum primum terris se *crastĭna* reddet. *Virg.*
> . . . . Mens tantum *pristĭna* mansit.   *Ovid.*

8. Diminutives in *olus, ola, olum,* and *ulus, ula, ulum,* shorten the penultimate; as, *urceŏlus, filiŏla, muscæŏlum; Lectŭlus, ratiŭncula, corculŭm,* &c.

Ante fugam soboles, si quis mihi *parvŭlus,* aula. *Virg.*

9. Adverbs in *tim* lengthen the penultimate; as, *oppidātim, diētim, virītim, tribūtim.*——Except *affătim* and

*perpĕtim;* also *stătim,* which has however been lengthened by poets living in an age of degenerate Latinity.

Et velut absentem *certātim* Actæona clamant. *Ovid.*
Stulta est fides celare quod prodas *stătim.*—(Iamb.)

10. Latin denominatives in *aceus, aneus, arius, aticus, orius;* also verbals in *abilis;* and words in *atilis,* whatever their derivation may be, lengthen their antepenultimate; as. *cretāceus, testāceus; momentāneus, subitāneus; cibārius, herbārius; aquāticus, fanāticus; censōrius, messōrius; amābilis, revocābilis; pluviātilis, plicātilis,* &c.

Aiunt, cum sibi sint congesta *cibāria,* sicut.   *Hor.*
Calcavêre pedis, nec solvit *aquāticus* Auster.   *Ovid.*

11. Adjectives in *icius,* derived from nouns, shorten the *i* of the antepenultimate; as, *gentilĭcius, patrĭcius, tribunĭcius.* Except *novĭcius,* or *novĭtius.* But those which come from supines or participles, lengthen the *i* of the antepenultimate; as, *advectīcius, commendatīcius, supposititīcius,* &c.

*Patrĭcios* omnes opibus cum provocet unus.   *Juv.*
Jam sedet in ripa, tetrumque *novĭcius* horret.   *Id.*
Hermes *supposititīcius* sibi ipsi.—(Phal.)   *Mart.*

12. Desideratives in *urio,* shorten the antepenultima, which in the second and third person is the penult; as, *esŭrio, esŭris, esŭrit.* But other verbs in *urio* lengthen that syllable; as, *ligūrio, ligūris; scatūrio, scatūris,* &c.

The quantity of the first and middle syllables of foreign or barbarous words introduced into the Latin language, cannot be determined, unless when they fall within the general rules.—Those first and middle syllables which cannot be ascertained by the preceding rules, must be determined by the practice or authority of the poets.

## SECTION IV.

#### OF PRONUNCIATION.

On this part of Latin *P*rosody it were needless to dilate, as the modes adopted in the pronunciation of the vowels, whether long or short, are so various, and so contradictory in various countries, and withal so firmly engrafted on their respective usages, that any attempt to lay down general rules would appear not only useless but presumptuous. The majority of classical scholars in all these countries where the study of Latin language and literature is cultivated, appear to concur in assigning to the vowels of that language, the same sound which they give the vowels of their own vernacular respectively. How absurd soever the custom may be, it is now too firmly fixed to admit a remedy: *nullis medicabilis* verbis.

In the Catholic Universities and Colleges, the mode adopted is that followed on the Continent of Europe; in the Literary Institutions of other denominations,—at least of those in the British empire and United States, the mode usually adopted, is that followed by the Universities of Oxford and Cambridge in England, and Trinity College, Dublin. In many institutions on either side of the Atlantic, both methods are, in some measure, blended with a preponderance, more or less, to either, according to the taste of the instructors, or the customs of the locality. The consequence is, that the stately and sonorous language of ancient Rome, for so many ages the most general medium of intercourse, written, printed, and oral, among the literati of all nations, is with much difficulty understood by a scholar of one country, when read in his hearing by the scholar of another! but when spoken in conversation it is scarcely intelligible!!*

---

\* Hence the sarcastic apology—for not answering in turn—made by *Scaliger*, when addressed in Latin by a Scotchman,—that "he" (*Scaliger*) "did not understand Gælic."

Without pretending to censure those who follow the modern improvements (?) in the mode of pronouncing the Latin words, the compiler ventures to offer a few words in defence of the mode, which he had been long taught to regard as that least liable to objection,—as nearest, in the majority of instances, to the pronunciation of the old Romans—and consequently as the best. He believes, then, that the sounds of the Latin vowels (long) ought to be nearly as laid down in the following scale:

The ā long like the English ā in *far;* as in the Latin words *Mārs, amāre.*
The ē     "           "        ē in *there;*   "        "         *diēs, tulēre.*
The ī     "           "        ī in *thine;*   "        "         *Nīlus, audīre.*
The ō     "           "        ō in *no;*      "        "         *timōre, nōlite.*
The ū     "           "        ū in *sure;*    "        "         *mūsa, dūco.*

Between the Latin *a* and the Greek *α* (ἄλφα) from which it had been derived, there could have been no essential difference of sound; being both pronounced when in combination, like the ā in *far;* as, *deārum, Mæcenās;* θεᾱ, ἀργός: but the foppish and finical sound of ā in *fate*, into which it has been metamorphosed by modern improvement, was certainly unknown to the full, open, *ore-rotundo* pronunciation of the stately lords of the world. To the majestic march and sonorous swell of "the long resounding line" in Latin verse, nothing probably has done more injury than this barbarous innovation.

The Latin ē, allowedly the η (ἦτα) of the Greeks, must have had a sound exactly similar to that of its primitive; like the English ē in *there;* or in the French words, *bête, tête;* as, in *aciēs, diēbus.* All doubt on the subject is removed by the testimony of Eustathius, who says that βῆ, βῆ, was a sound formed from the bleating of sheep; quoting the well known verse of the poet:

Ὁ δ' ἠλίθιος, ὥσπερ πρόβατον, βῆ, βῆ λέγων βαδίζει:

so that the modernized, attenuated sound of ē in *wē*,

foisted on this vowel, had been wholly unknown to the ancients.

The vowel $\bar{\imath}$ being the Latin representative of the Greek proper diphthong ει,—not of the vowel ι (ίῶτα), as some assert,—must be supposed to have preserved the sound of both letters, and to have been pronounced like the English $\bar{\imath}$ in *thīne* ;* as, *Nīlus*, (the river), *Iphigenīa*, *dīcere*.† Victorinus shows that the quantity of $\bar{\imath}$ was marked by the ancients as if *ei* diphthong: which is also proved from Lucilius where alluding to the sound of $\bar{\imath}$ in the plural of words, he says—

*Jam puerei venere ē postremum facito atque ī*
*Hoc illei fecere, addes ē ut pinguius fiat :—*

"That it may become fuller;" an observation by no means applicable to the sound of $\bar{e}$, into which it has been too generally converted.‡

In $\bar{o}$, from the Greek ω (ώμέγα)—more fortunate than its brethren,—scarcely any difference has *yet* appeared between the two systems alluded to above; all agreeing to give it the sound assigned it by nature, that of the English $\bar{o}$ in *nō, ōh;* in French *côte*, and the Latin words *mōbilis, pōculum;* agreeably to the quantity of the Greek vowel whence derived.

In $\bar{u}$, from the Greek υ (ύψιλόν), the difference between the two systems has, in all probability, been as great as in the case of the vowel $\bar{\imath}$;—the scholars on the Continent generally giving it the sound of *u* in *rūle* ($\bar{oo}$), while those of the British empire most commonly pronounce it like the English $\bar{u}$ in *sūre, tūbe ;* as in *manū, cornū :—*a

---

* It must not, however, be concealed, that this opinion is different from that of many learned Prosodians.

† The force of custom has been more than usually capricious in the use or abuse of this letter; not unfrequently compelling the bewildered student to follow two different modes of pronunciation in the same line; as—
 *Cūi tu lăcte favos et miti dīlue Baccho.* Virg.

‡ Qu.—Perverted!

sound far preferable, not only from its more uniform prevalence in the recitation of the language, but from its greater fullness and expressiveness : yet it must in candor be admitted, that the sound given by the scholars of the Continent of Europe, approximates more closely to that *supposed* to be the sound of the ancient Romans than the one adopted by the scholars of the British empire; for although derived from the Greek *v* (ὑψιλόν), the Latin *ū* would appear to have differed widely from its primitive : whence Ausonius tells us, that the sound of the Roman *u* " had been unknown to the Greeks"—*Cecropiis ignota:* and Plautus makes his Parasite say—

*Tu, tu, illic inquam, vin' adferri noctuam—*

comparing it to the note or hooting of the owl.

With regard to the partial adoption of both systems, the natural result is, the absence of all consistency : whereas those who strenuously insist on the mincing *petit-maitre* sound of *a* and *e*, as in the English vowels in *fāte* and *mē*, almost uniformly abandon the sound of the English vowels in the case of *i;* and generally in that of *ū ;*— pronouncing the former as *ē* and the latter as *ōō !* If the Latin vowels *ā* and *ē* are doomed to submit to the Saxon yoke, why exempt *ī* and *ū ?* If *ī* (sounded as *ē*) and *ū* (sounded as *ōō*) are retained as agreeable to the method of the Romans, why not retain *ā* and *ē*, as unquestionably pronounced by the same people, and as given in the above scale ? In our improvements, let us preserve some appearance at least of consistency. Let us Anglicize all or Latinize all : but let us not blunder like the foolish painter in Horace—

*Ut nec pes nec caput uni*
*Reddatur formæ.*

## SECTION V.

#### FIGURES OF PROSODY,

Are sixteen: viz. 1. Cæsura; 2. Synæresis (with its two co-relatives, Crasis and Synecphonesis); 3. Diæresis, or Dialysis; 4. Elision, (divided into Synalœpha and Ecthlipsis); 5. Systole; 6. Diastole or Ectasis; 7. Synapheia; 8. Prothesis; 9. Aphæresis; 10. Syncope; 11. Epenthesis; 12. Apocope; 13. Paragoge; 14. Tmesis; 15. Antithesis; and 16. Metathesis.

#### 1. Cæsura.*

The term Cæsura is used by Prosodians in two different acceptations:—1st, as applied to whole verses, and 2d, as applied to single feet. Lines in poetry are most generally so constructed, that the voice of the reader is naturally required to make a short pause or rest at that part of every line or verse, where it can be most conveniently done without injury to the sense or the harmony of the line, as,

*Tantæ molis erat‖Romanam condere gentem.*
*Errabant acti fatis‖maria omnia circum.*

The division thus produced by the halt or pause is called *Cæsura—Cæsural Pause*, or perhaps more correctly—*Lineal Cæsura*. This is the term in its first acceptation, and is used chiefly in reference to Hexameter verse. It shall be noticed again under the rules for the construction of Latin verse.

Cæsura in its second application occurs in the manner following: viz., when a foot is made up of syllables belonging to separate consecutive words, and when the first

---

* From *cadere*, " to cut " or "divide."

syllable of that foot is the last syllable of the preceding word, then the space, separation, or division between the two consecutive words, is called *Cæsura* simply; or more emphatically, the *Metrical Cæsura;* as referring to a foot or measure; thus in the following line,

Pāstō|rēs ŏvĭ|ūm tĕnĕr|ōs dē|pēllĕrĕ fœtūs—

the Metrical Cæsura occurs three times—in the second foot, *rēs ŏvĭ*, where the division takes place between *rēs* and *ŏvĭ;*—in the third foot *ūm tĕnĕr*, where it takes place between *ūm* and *tĕnĕr;*—in fourth foot *ōs dē*, where it takes place between *ōs* and *dē*.

Of Metrical Cæsura, there are three kinds; namely, the *Syllabic*, the *Trochaic*, and the *Monosyllabic*.

The *Syllabic Cæsura* is that, in which the first part of the divided foot consists of the last syllable of the preceding word; as the syllables *res*, *um*, and *os* of the line just quoted.

The *Syllabic Cæsura* may take place in five positions; viz., after the first syllable of the 2d, 3d, 4th, 5th, or 6th foot: or in the technical language of *P*rosodians, the Cæsura after the 1st syllable of the 2d foot is called *Triemimeris*, that is, "of the third half foot;" that after the 1st syllable of the third foot, or 5th half foot, is called *Penthemimeris;*—at the 7th semi-foot, *Hephthemimeris;* —at the 9th, *Enneemimeris;*—and at the 11th semi-foot, or 1st syllable of the last foot, *Hendecemimeris.** This Cæsura (the *Hendecemimeris*) never occurs unless where the last word is a monosyllable.

EXAMPLES TO ELUCIDATE THE FOREGOING DEFINITIONS.

1. Pectori|*bus* inhi|ans spi|rantia | consulit | exta.

---

* These terms are formed of ἡμι "half," and μερός or μερίς "part," with the Greek numerals prefixed.

2. Emicat Eurya|*lŭs* ☞ et | munere | victor a|mici.

3. Una ea|demque vi|a san|*guĭs* ☞ ani|musque se|quuntur.

4. Graius ho|mo infec|tos lin|quens profu|*gŭs* ☞ hyme|nœos.

5. Vertitur | intere|a cœ|lum et ruit | Ocea|*nō* ☞ nox.

The ☞ points out the position of the Cæsura in each line, viz., of the *Triemimeris* after *bus;* of the *Penthemimeris* after *lus;*—of the *Hephthemimeris* after *guis;*—of the *Enneemimeris* after *gus;*—of the *Hendecemimeris* after *no;* or as expressed in the following tabular form:—

|         |                   |                |           |                 |
|---------|-------------------|----------------|-----------|-----------------|
| The Cæsura | in the 2d foot | or 3d half foot | is called | Triemimeris.    |
|         | "  3d  "          | or 5th    "    |           | Penthemimeris.  |
|         | "  4th "          | or 7th    "    |           | Hephthemimeris. |
|         | "  5th "          | or 9th    "    |           | Enneemimeris.   |
|         | "  6th "          | or 11th   "    |           | Hendecemimeris. |

Of these pauses or rests, the most beautiful—as tending beyond all others to impart sweetness, smoothness, and rythm to the verse,—is that which occurs after the *Penthemimeris.* The pause after *Triemimeris* and *Hephthemimeris,* are also ornamental, though in a less degree; but the *Enneemimeris* and *Hendecemimeris* are injurious to harmony, and are to be sparingly used; unless where the want of smoothness may be desirable.

The *Trochaic Cæsura* is that, in which the first part of the divided foot consists of either a long and short syllable (a trochee ¯ ˘) remaining at the end of a word, or of an an entire word comprised of a long and a short syllable (a trochee); as,

Fōrtū|*nātŭs* ĕt | *illĕ* dĕ|ōs quī|*nōvĭt* ă|grēstēs. *Virg.*

Here *nātŭs* in the 2d foot, *illĕ* in the third, and *nōvĭt* in the 5th, form, each a trochee, and at each of these divisions, the *Trochaic Cæsura* occurs.

The *Trochaic Cæsura* may occur in any of the first five feet of a verse; as,

Tālĭă | *vōcĕ* rĕ|fērt, ō|*tērquĕ* qŭa|*tērquĕ* bĕ|ātī. *Virg.*
Ārmă prŏ|cūl cūr|*rūsque* vĭ|rūm mī|*rātŭr* ĭn|ānēs. *Id.*

The syllables in *Italics* point out the Cæsura.

Two successive trochees in the 2d and 3d feet should be avoided; as they give the verse a flippant, cantering air or manner, which is extremely inelegant and undignified; as,

Ērgŏ mă|*gĭsquĕ* mă|*gĭsquĕ* vĭ|rī nūnc|glōrĭă|clārēt. *En.*

The *Monosyllabic Cæsura* is that, in which the first syllable of the divided foot, is a monosyllable; as,

Hĭc vĭr hĭc|*ēst* tĭbĭ|*quēm* prŏ|mīttī|sæpĭŭs|aūdīs. *Virg.*

Of the three kinds of Cæsura, the principal is the *Syllabic*; the next in metrical effect is the *Trochaic*; but the *Monosyllabic* is inferior to either, and yet, in many instances, it would appear to be the principal Cæsura in the verse.

ON THE LENGTHENING POWER OF THE CÆSURA.

*Syllaba sæpe brevis Cæsurâ extenditur, etsi
Litera nec duplex nec consona bina sequatur.*

A short syllable in the Cæsura is frequently made long, although its vowel may not be followed by two consonants or a double letter.

Instead of attributing this to the power of the Cæsura, it is more agreeable to the laws of metre to ascribe it to the halt, pause, or suspension of the voice invariably accompanied by what is called the *ictus*, which takes place at the division of the foot, and which being counted into the time or duration of the preceding short syllable, makes it long:—the Cæsural pause producing an effect similar to that of the final pause. Again, the swell or stress of the voice in dactylic versification invariably falling on the first syllable* of the foot, produces the same effect on that syllable, as if its final letter were pronounced *double;* the voice striking emphatically and dwelling forcibly, for an instant, on the latter of the double letters.†

2.—SYNÆRESIS,‡ with its two co-relatives, CRASIS§ and SYNECPHONESIS.‖

*Syllaba, de gemina facta una,* Synæresis *esto.*

Two vowels naturally forming separate syllables, but read and pronounced as one syllable, form a *Synæresis;* as, *a-i-o,* pronounced *ai-o.*

EXAMPLES BY SINGLE WORDS.

*Pro-in-de, pro-hi-be-at, Tro-i-a, a-i-unt,* &c., pronounced *prōin-de, prōi-be-at, Trōi-a, āi-unt.*

EXAMPLES IN COMPOSITION.

Proinde *tona eloquio, solitum tibi; meque timoris.* Virg.

making a diphthong of the two contiguous vowels in the word *Pro-in-de,—Prōin-de,* and preserving the sound of

---

\* Called the ἄρσις or "elevation;"—the tone being here always more elevated: the other part being called θέσις or "depression;" this part of the foot being comparatively depressed.

† To render this familiar to the young Prosodian, he should be taught to read the Cæsural syllables in the five verses given above, with a strong emphasis, as if written *Pectoribu*SS, *Euryalu*SS, *Sangui*SS, *Profugu*SS, &c., forcibly, although momentarily, dwelling on the duplicated letter. Servius on Æneid, 3, 91, says the syllable is made long *finalitatis ratione:* and Quintilian, Lib. 9, c. 4, agrees that—*in ipsa divisione verborum* (the Cæsura) *quoddam latens tempus.*

‡ From συναίρεσις, "a contraction."

§ From κρᾶσις, "a mixture" or "blending."

‖ From συνεκφώνησις, "a mutation of sound."

both. This seems the peculiar province of *Synæresis*, as the other contractions and alterations attributed to this figure, more properly come under the head of *Crasis* and *Synecphonesis*.

### CRASIS,

Blends or runs two vowels into one, so that the sound of one at least is lost; as, *pro-emo—pro-mo*.

#### EXAMPLES BY SINGLE WORDS.

*E-a-dem* (*eadem*), *co-al-u-e-rint* (*coaluerint*), *al-ve-a-ri-a* (*alvearia*), &c.,—pronounced *adem, co-luerint, alvaria*, &c.

#### EXAMPLES IN COMPOSITION.

*Seu lento fuerint* alvearia *vimine texta.* Virg.

To *Crasis* then—as the name indicates—properly belongs all contractions, where the sound of one of the two contiguous vowels is lost.

### SYNECPHONESIS,

Is the change of a vowel sound into that of a consonant; as, of *I* and of *U* into the sound of *J* and *V*, (or *W*); as, *parietibus*, pronounced *par-yetibus*.

#### EXAMPLES BY SINGLE WORDS.

*Genua, tenuis, pituita, tuas, fortuito*, &c.,—pronounced *gen-va* or *wa, ten-vis* or *-wis, pit-wita, twas, fort-wito*, &c.

#### EXAMPLES IN COMPOSITION.

*Hærent* parietibus *scala, postesque, sub ipsos.* Virg.

### 3.—DIÆRESIS,* or DIALYSIS.†

*Distrahit in geminas resoluta* Diæresis *unam.*

A *Diæresis* is the division of one syllable into two; as *auraï* for *auræ*.

---

\* From διαίρεσις, "a division."
† From διάλυσις, "a loosening."

## FIGURES OF PROSODY.

#### EXAMPLES BY SINGLE WORDS.

*Silŭa* (for *silva*), *solŭa* (for *solvo*), *suädent* (for *suadent*), *Tro-i-a* (for *Troi-a*), *Ecquïs* (for *Ecquis*.)

#### EXAMPLES IN COMPOSITION.

*Æthereum sensum, atque* auraï *simplicis ignem.* Virg.

4.—ELISION\* is divided in Synalœpha† and Ecthlipsis.‡

### 1. SYNALŒPHA.

*Dipthongum aut vocalem haurit* Synalœpha *priorem.*

*Synalœpha* is the elision (or cutting off) of a vowel or diphthong at the end of a word, when the following word begins with a vowel or diphthong, or the letter *h;* as, *conticuer' omnes,* for *conticuere omnes.*

#### EXAMPLES BY SINGLE WORDS.

*Intentiqu' ora* (for *intentique ora*) *Dardanid' e muris* (for *Dardanidæ e muris*), *ub' ingens* (for *'ubi ingens*), *atqu' yemes* (for *atque hyemes*.)

#### EXAMPLES IN COMPOSITION.

*Quidve moror?* si omnes uno ordine *habetis Achivos.* Vir.

This line must be scanned thus :—

*Quidve moror?* s'omnes un' ordin' *habetis Achivos.*

### 2. ECTHLIPSIS.

M *vorat* Ecthlipsis, *quoties vocalibus anteit.*

*Ecthlipsis* cuts off the final *m* and the preceding vowel,§ when the following word begins with a vowel; as, *virtut' ex* for *virtutem ex.*

---
\* From *elisio* (wh. fr. *elidēre*), "a cutting off."
† From συναλοιφή, "a coalescing," or rather "a re-anointing or smearing over, to conceal or destroy the last coat or layer."
‡ From ἔκθλιψις, "a striking out."
§ The preceding vowel is—to speak accurately—thus cut off by the Synalœpha, on the removal of the *m*.

## FIGURES OF PROSODY.

#### EXAMPLES BY SINGLE WORDS.

*O ! quant' est* for *O ! quantum est*) *tec' una* (for *tecum una*), *ferend' est* (for *ferendum est*).

#### EXAMPLES IN COMPOSITION.

*Disce, puer, virtut*em *ex me, verumque laborem.*
*Fortun*am *ex aliis.*                          Virg.

### 5.—Systole.*

Systole *præcipitat positu vel origine longam.*

*Systole* shortens a syllable otherwise long by nature or by position; as, *vidĕn'* for *vidēsne*.

#### EXAMPLES BY SINGLE WORDS.

*Stetĕrunt, tulĕrunt, hŏdie* (for *hōc-die*), *ŏbicis* (for *ōbjicis*), *ŏmitto* (for *ōbmitto*).

#### EXAMPLES IN COMPOSITION.

*Cum subitò assurgens fluctu nimbosus Ŏrion.*†     Virg.

### 6.—Diastole,‡ or Ectasis.§

*Ectasis extenditque brevem, duplicatque elementum.*

By *Ectasis* a syllable naturally short is made long; as, *ītalia* for *ĭtalia :* it sometimes doubles the consonant; as, *rēlligio* for *rĕligio*.

#### EXAMPLES BY SINGLE WORDS.

*Relliquiæ, repperit, Prīamides* (from *Prĭamus*), *Ārabia*, (from *Ărabs*).

#### EXAMPLES IN COMPOSITION.

*Qui clypeo, galeaque,* Macēdonia*que, sarissa.*    Ovid.

---

\* From συστολή, "a contraction, or shortening."

☞ For the objections urged against the existence of Systole, the curious student should read Carey, Anthon and others, under this head.

† Written in Greek with an ω, and consequently long by nature, it is here shortened by the figure.

‡ From διαστολή, "an extension," or "lengthening."

§ From ἔκτασις, the same.

### 7.—SYNAPHEIA.*

*Copulat irrupto versus* Synapheia *tenore.*

**Synapheia** connects verses together, in such a manner as to make them run on uninterruptedly, as if not divided into separate lines or verses. By this mode of connecting lines together—*irrupto tenore*—the *initial* syllable of a succeeding verse has an influence on the *final* syllable of the preceding,—affecting it by the concourse of consonants, by ecthlipsis, and by synalœpha. The use of synapheia was however confined principally to anapæstic verse and the Ionic *a minore.* In other species of verse, it was rarely introduced by any of the great poets.

The following anapæstic lines are examples of **Synapheia:**

*Prǣcēps|sȳlvās‖mōntēs|quĕ fŭgĭt‖*
*Cĭtŭs Āct|ǣŏn,‖ăgĭlĭs|quĕ măgĭs‖*
*Pĕdĕ pēr|sāltŭs‖ēt sāx|ā văgŭs‖*
*Mĕtŭĭt|mōtās‖Zĕphȳrĭs|plūmās.‖*   Seneca.

By reading these lines—*continuo carmine*—the naturally *short* final syllables of *fŭgĭt, măgĭs,* and *văgŭs,* respectively become *long* by position before their own final, and the initial consonants in the lines immediately succeeding.

Virgil's hexameters also furnish some examples; as—

*Jactemur, doceas: ignari hominumque locorum|*que
*Erramus, vento huc et vastis fluctibus acti.*

In this example the first line ends with *rum,* the superfluous syllable *que* at the termination, combines with *Er* the first syllable in the second line, and thence by *Synapheia* and *Synalœpha,* produces *Qu'ērrā,*—as a spondee, to commence the second line.*

---

\* From συναφεία, "a conjunction, or joining together."
† The celebrated Bentley, in his *Dissertation upon Phalaris,* had the merit of discovering the law of Synapheia.

## FIGURES OF PROSODY.

### 8.—Prosthesis.* 9.—Aphæresis.†

*Principium apponit* Prosthesis, *quod* Aphæresis *aufert.*

*Prosthesis* adds a letter or syllable to the beginning of a word; while *Aphæresis* takes away a letter or syllable from it. *Examples of Prosthesis—Gnatus* for *Natus; Tetuli* for *Tuli:—of Aphæresis—'st* for *est, Camander* and *Maragdus* for *Scamander* and *Smaragdus.*

EXAMPLES IN COMPOSITION—OF APHÆRESIS.

*Tu poteras virides pennis hebetare* smaragdos.‡ Ovid.

### 10.—Syncope.§ 11.—Epenthesis.‖

Syncope *de medio tollit, quod* Epenthesis *addit.*

*Syncope* takes away a letter or syllable from the middle of a word, while *Epenthesis* adds it. *Examples of Syncope.—Periclum* (for *Periculum*), *Pænûm* (for *Pænorum*), *aspris* (for *asperis*), *audiit* (for *audivit*):—*of Epenthesis.—Redeo* (for *re-eo*), *seditio* (for *se-itio*), *pluvi* (for *plui*).

EXAMPLES IN COMPOSITION—OF SYNCOPE.

*Cingite fronde comas, et pocula* porgite¶ *dextris.* Virg.

### 12.—Apocope.** 13.—Paragoge.††

Apocope *demit finem, quem dat* Paragoge.

*Apocope* strikes off, while *Paragoge* adds, a final letter or syllable.

*Examples of Apocope.* Men' (for *mene*), tuguri (for

---

\* From πρόσθεσις, "an addition."
† From ἀφαίρεσις, "a taking away."
‡ Where the initial *s* is not pronounced.
§ From συγκόπη, "a cutting away."
‖ From ἐπένθεσις, "an insertion."
¶ *Porgite*—for *porrigite.*
\*\* From ἀποκόπη, "a cutting off."
†† From παραγωγή, "a bringing into."

*tugurii*), *neu* (for *neve*) :—*of* Paragoge—*Deludier* (for *deludi, legier* (for *legi*), *amarier* (for *amari*).

### EXAMPLES IN COMPOSITION—OF PARAGOGE.

*At Venulus, dicto parens, ita* farier\* *infit.*   Virg.

### 14.—Tmesis.†

*Per* Tmesim *inseritur medio vox altera vocis.*

Tmesis is the separation of a word into two parts, for the insertion of another word between the parts divided.

### EXAMPLES BY SINGLE WORDS.

*Qui* te *cumque* (for quicunque te), *Septem* subjecta *Trioni* (for Septemtrioni).

### EXAMPLES IN COMPOSITION.

*Talis* Hyperboreo Septem *subjecta* trioni.   Virg.

### 15.—Antithesis.‡   16.—Metathesis.§

*Nonnunquam* Antithesi *mutatur litera, ut* olli;
*Cum propria migrat de sede,* Metathesis *esto.*

Antithesis substitutes one letter for another; as *olli* for *illi:* while Metathesis changes the order of the letters in a word; as, *Thymbre* for *Thymber.*

### EXAMPLES BY SINGLE WORDS.

Of *Antithesis.*—*Faciundum* for *faciendum, Publicus* for *Poplicus*—*Populicus, Vult,* for *volt, adsum* for *assum,* &c.: of *Metathesis*—*Corcodilus* for *Crocodilus, extremus* for *exterrimus*—by syncope, *exter'mus, supremus* for *superrimus*—by syncope, *super'mus,* &c.

---

\* For *fari.*
† From τμῆσις, "a cutting or incision."
‡ From ἀντίθεσις, "a substitution."
§ From μετάθεσις, "a transposition."

## EXAMPLES IN COMPOSITION—OF METATHESIS.

*Tu quoque cognosces in me*, Meleagre,* *sororem.* Ovid.

### OBSERVATIONS.

Although most of the foregoing figures of Prosody may be considered imaginary, being, in reality, nothing more, than so many Archaisms, Anomalies, or Poetic Licenses, still it was deemed necessary, in compliance with custom—

*Quem penes arbitrium est, et jus et norma loquendi—*

to give them place, as conducive to the perfection of the plan proposed in this little work; particularly, as the curious reader will, in the course of his studies, find these figures, on most occasions, treated of under their proper appellations by the most learned Grammarians, Prosodians, and Commentators.

## SECTION VI.

### OF VERSIFICATION.

1. Poems (*carmina*) are composed of verses or lines; verses are composed of feet,† and feet of syllables. A

---

* For *Meleager*.
† Feet in metre are thus denominated, because the voice appears by their aid, to move along in measured pace, through the verse. Foot as applied to poetry may also be thus derived:—According to Marius Victorinus, arsis was the noiseless raising of the foot—*Sublatio pedis sine sono,*—while thesis was the dropping of it, audibly striking the ground—*positio pedis cum sono :*—observing also, that it was not so much by the number of syllables, as by the time, the arsis and thesis were regulated. Horace himself, and after him Terentianus Maurus, allude to this method of distinguishing the feet: keeping time according to the arsis and thesis, by the tapping of the thumb or the beating of the foot—

Lesbium servate *pedem,* meique
*Pollicis ictum.* Lib. iv. Ode vi.

Verse is so called from turning back (*vertendo*); because when the line is completed by the requisite number of syllables, we turn back to the beginning of another line. By the Greeks, it was called στίχος, " order " or " rank," from the disposition of the lines. From στίχος. and ἥμισυς, " the half," comes hemistich, or half verse. The term hemistich is also usually applied to either portions of a line or verse divided at the penthemimeris; as,—

*Ære ciere viros*‖*Martemque accendere cantu.* Virg.

foot, then, is a combination of syllables employed in measuring verse.

2. Feet are either *simple* or *compound*. *Simple* feet consist of two or three syllables; *compound* feet are formed by joining together two simple feet.

3. All the possible combinations of two syllables are four;—of three syllables, eight;—and of four syllables, sixteen: making twenty-eight different kinds. To these some Prosodians add two other compound feet of five syllables; viz.,—the Dochimus or Dochmius, and Mesomacer: making thirty in all.

### SIMPLE FEET OF TWO SYLLABLES.

1. The SPONDEE\* (*Spondæus*) consists of two long syllables; as, ōmnēs.

2. The PYRRHICH† (*Pyrrhichius*) consists of two short syllables; as, dĕŭs.

3. The TROCHEE‡ (*Trochæus*) consists of one long and one short syllable; as, sērvăt.

4. The IAMBUS§ (*Iambus*) consists of one short and one long syllable; as, pĭōs.

### SIMPLE FEET OF THREE SYLLABLES.

1. The MOLOSSUS‖ (*Molossus*) consists of three long syllables; as, dēlēctānt.

---

\* Derived from σπονδή, "a libation," being originally used from its majestic gravity, in the slow solemn chant at sacrifices.

† So called, from πυρρίχη, "a martial dance" performed by armed men, in which this quick and lively measure was predominant. Some derive it from Pyrrhus, son of Achilles, as the inventor; while others attribute it to Pyrrhicus, the Cydonian.

‡ Supposed to be derived from τρέχειν, "to run,"—τροχός, "a wheel," from its lively movement. By the Greeks it was also called χορεῖος, (from χόρος, "a dance") and by the Latins *Choræus*, from its adaptation for dancing.

§ From ἰάπτειν, "to rail against; because this foot was first used in satirical compositions. Others derive it from the nymph *Iumbé*, by whom it was used in singing for Ceres to alleviate her grief for the loss of Proserpina.

‖ After *Molossus*, son of Pyrrhus and Andromache, who used to sing hymns composed in this metre, before the shrine of Dodona; or, as others say, from its being used in the war songs of the *Molossi*, a people of Epirus.

# VERSIFICATION.

2. The TRIBRACH* (*Tribrăchys*) consists of three short syllables; as, *mĕlĭŭs*.

3. The DACTYL† (*Dactylus*) consists of one long and two short; as *cărmĭnă*.

4. The ANAPÆST‡ (*Anapæstus*) consists of two short syllables and one long one; as, *ănĭmōs*.

5. The BACCHIUS§ (*Βακχεῖος*) consists of one short syllable followed by two long ones; as, *dŏlōrēs*.

6. The ANTIBACCHIUS‖ (*Ἀντιβακχεῖος*) consists of two long syllables followed by a short one; as, *pēllūntŭr*.

7. The AMPHIMACER¶ (*Ἀμφίμακρος*) consists of one short syllable between two long ones; as, *cāstĭtās*.

8. The AMPHIBRACH** (*Amphibrachys*) consists of one long syllable between two short ones; as, *ămārĕ*.

## COMPOUND FEET.

1. The DISPONDÆUS, or Double Spondee, is composed of four long syllables, or two spondees; as, *īnfīnītīs*.

2. The PROCELEUSMATICUS†† is composed of two pyrrhichs, or four short syllables; as, *hŏmĭnĭbŭs*.

---

\* From τρεῖς, "three" and βραχύς, "short." It is also called *Choreus*, and by Quintilian, *Trochæus*.

† From δάκτυλος, "a finger;" which has one long joint and two short ones. Some derive it *ab Idæis Dactylis*, by whom this metre was used in the songs and music played and sung to drown the cries of the infant Jupiter, while being concealed on Ida from the child-devouring Saturn. By others it was called *Heroüs*, from its use in describing heroic achievements.

‡ From ἀναπαίω, "I strike or beat in reverse order;" because those who danced according to the cadence of this foot, used to beat the ground in a manner different from those observing the dactylic movement. Hence it was also called Ἀντιδάκτυλος (*Antidactylus*) by the Greeks, and *Retroactus* by the Latins.

§ So called from its frequent use in hymns to Bacchus.

‖ From its being used in opposition to the Bacchius; in the same way probably as the *Anapæst* and the *Dactyl*.

¶ From ἀμφί, "on both sides," and μακρός, "long." ☞ This foot is also called CRETIC; (*Creticus*) and is then derived from the fancied similarity between this measure and the time observed by the Corybantes of Crete when striking on their shields or cymbals to drown the cries of the infant Jupiter; as already mentioned in the note on the DACTYL.

** From ἀμφί, "on both sides," and βραχύς, "short."

†† From κέλευσμα, "the word of command" given by the leader of a choir or dance, which was performed in double quick time. Others derive it from the

## VERSIFICATION.

3. The Dïambus, or Double Iambus, consists of two iambi; as, *sĕvērĭtās*.

4. The Ditrochæus, or Dichoræus, consists of two trochees; as, *pērmănērĕ*.

5. The Ionĭcus Major (or *a Majōre*) consists of a spondee and a pyrrhic—two long and two short; as, *cālcārĭbŭs*.

6. The Ionĭcus Minor (or *a Minōre*) consists of a pyrrhich and a spondee—two short and two long; as, *prŏpĕrābānt*.*

7. The Choriambus consists of a choræus or trochæus, and an iambus—two short between two long; as, *nōbĭlĭtās*.

8. The Antispast† (*Antispastus*) consists of an iambus and a trochee—two long between two short; as, *sĕcūndārĕ*.

9. The Epitrĭtus Primus, or First Epitrit, consists of an iambus and a spondee—one short and three long; as, *sălūtāntēs*.

10. The Epitrĭtus Secundus, or Second Epitrit, consists of a trochee and a spondee—a long, a short, and two long; as, *cōncĭtātī*.

11. The Epitrĭtus Tertius, or Third Epitrit, consists of a spondee and an iambus—two long with a short and a long; as, *cōmmūnĭcānt*.

12. The Epitrĭtus Quartus,‡ or Fourth Epitrit, con-

---

word given out by the master or captain of a vessel to encourage his crew to greater exertion and celerity.

* These two are called Ionic, from their use among the Ionians. One is called *a majore*, because it begins with the greater quantity—two long: the other is called *a minore*, because it begins with the less, that is, with two short syllables. Some authors think these measures were so called from *Ion*, their inventor.

† From ἀντισπᾶσθαι, "to be drawn asunder;" two long syllables being separated or drawn asunder by two short ones.

‡ These four derive their name from ἐπί, "beyond," and τρίτος, "the third;"

sists of a spondee and a trochee—three long and one short; as, *incāntārĕ*.

13. The P*æ*on P*rimus*, or First Pæon, consists of a trochee and a pyrrhich—one long and three short; as, *cōnfĭcĕrĕ*.

14. The P*æ*on S*ecundus*, or Second Pæon, consists of an iambus and a pyrrhich—a short, a long, and two short; as, *rĕsōlvĕrĕ*.

15. The P*æ*on T*ertius*, or Third Pæon, consists of a pyrrhich and a trochee—two short, a long and a short; as, *sŏcĭārĕ*.

16. The P*æ*on Q*uartus*,* or Fourth Pæon, consists of a pyrrhich and an iambus—three short and one long; as, *cĕlĕrĭtās*.

1. The D*ochmius*† (*Δόχμιος*) consists of an Antispast and a long syllable—a short, two long, a short and a long; as, *ăbērrāvĕrānt*.

2. The M*esomacer*‡ (*Μεσόμακρος*) consists of a pyrrhich and a dactyl—two short, a long, and two short; as, *ăvĭdīssĭmŭs*.

---

because they have three measures and something more; then they are called first, second, third, and fourth, from the relative situation of the short syllable.

* The name of these four is, by some authors, derived from *Pæon*, its inventor. Others, however, with more plausibility, derive it from Apollo; to whose honour, hymns were composed and sung in this measure. Similar to other metres, the Pæon is the opposite to the Epitrit; whereas in the latter there is one short with three long, but in the former there is one long with three short. Thus, also, the first, second, third, and fourth Pæons are so named from the relative position of the long syllable in each.

† From *δόχμιος*, "oblique or irregular," on account of its irregularity and deviation from the customary laws of metre.

‡ From *μέσος*, "middle," and *μακρός*, "from the position of the long in the midst of two short on each side.

# A TABLE OF THE VARIOUS KINDS OF FEET USED IN THE COMPOSITION OF LATIN VERSE.

☞ To assist the memory in distinguishing the feet from one another, the pupil should be taught to observe the order represented in the following table, and also to remark the contrariety or opposition subsisting in each couplet. Thus in the first couplet, the spondee is composed of *two long* syllables, and the Pyrrhich of *two short*; in the next, the Choree is *one long and one short*; while the Iambus is *one short and one long*; and so on throughout.

*There are Thirty Feet, Twelve Simple, and Eighteen Compound.*

## 1. TWELVE SIMPLE FEET, of which Four are Dissyllables, Eight Trisyllables.

### Four Feet of Two Syllables.

1. { A Spondee (*Spondæus*, or *Spondeus*) — two long syllables, as — Mūsām
2. { A Pyrrhic (*Pyrrhicus*, or *Pyrrhichius*) — two short — Dĕŭs
3. { A Choree, or Trochee (*Choreus*, or *Trochæus*) — one long, one short — Māgnŭs
4. { An Iambus (*Iambus*) — one short, one long — Lĕgūnt

### Eight Feet of Three Syllables.

5. { A Molossus (*Molossus*) — three long — Dīxērūnt
6. { A Tribrac (*Tribrachys*) — three short — Hŏmĭnĕ
7. { A Dactyl (*Dactylus*) — one long, two short — Cārmĭnĕ
8. { An Anapest (*Anapæstus*) — two short, one long — Lĕgĕrēnt
9. { A Bacchic (*Bacchius*) — one short, two long — Lĕgēbānt
10. { An Antibacchic or Palimbacchic (*Antibacchius, &c.*) — two long, one short — Aūdīrĕ
11. { A Cretic, or Amphimacer (*Creticus, &c.*) — one short between two long — Cāstĭtās
12. { An Amphibrac (*Amphibrachys*) — one long between two short — Rĕmōtŭs

2 EIGHTEEN COMPOUND FEET, of which sixteen are of four Syllables, and two of five. Of the first sixteen, four are of the same Foot doubled; four of contrary Feet; four, in which long Times predominate; and four, in which short Times predominate.

### Four of the same Foot doubled.

| | | | |
|---|---|---|---|
| 13 | A Dispondee (*Dispondæus*) | two Spondees | Incrēmēntŭm |
| 14 | A Proceleusmatic (*Proceleusmaticus*) | two Pyrrhics | Hŏmĭnĭbŭs |
| 15 | A Dichoree (*Dichoreus*) | two Chorees | Cōmprŏbāvĭt |
| 16 | A Diiambus (*Diiambus*) | two Iambuses | Amœnĭtās |

### Four of contrary Feet.

| | | | |
|---|---|---|---|
| 17 | A great Ionic (*Major Ionicus*) | a Spondee and a Pyrrhic | Cēlsĭssĭmŭs |
| 18 | A small Ionic (*Minor Ionicus*) | a Pyrrhic and a Spondee | Dĭŏmēdēs |
| 19 | A Choriambus (*Choriambus*) | a Choree and Iambus | Hĭstŏrĭās |
| 20 | An Antispast (*Antispastus*) | an Iambus and Choree | Rĕmŏvērē |

### Four Feet in which long Times exceed.

| | | | |
|---|---|---|---|
| 21 | First Epitrit (*Epitritus Primus*) | an Iambus and Spondee | Vŏlūptātĭs |
| 22 | Second Epitrit (*Ep. Sec.*) | a Choree and Spondee | Cōncĭtārī |
| 23 | Third Epitrit (*Ep. Tert.*) | a Spondee and Iambus | Cōmmūnĭcās |
| 24 | Fourth Epitrit (*Ep. Quartus*) | a Spondee and Choree | Expēctārē |

### Four Feet in which short Times exceed.

| | | | |
|---|---|---|---|
| 25 | First Pæon, or Pæan (*Pæon Primus*) | a Choree and Pyrrhic | Præcĭpĕrĕ |
| 26 | Second Pæon (*Pæon Sec.*) | an Iambus and Pyrrhic | Rĕsōlvĕrĕt |
| 27 | Third Pæon (*Pæon Tertius*) | a Pyrrhic and Choree | Ălĭēnŭs |
| 28 | Fourth Pæon (*Pæon Quartus*) | a Pyrrhic and Iambus | Tĕmĕrĭtās |

### Two other compound Feet of Five Syllables.

| | | | |
|---|---|---|---|
| 29 | Dochimius or Dochmius (*Cic and Quinctil.*) | an Iambus and Cretic | Ĭn ārmĭs fŭī |
| 30 | Mesomacer (*Scaliger & Vossius*) | a Pyrrhic and a Dactyl | Prŏhĭbēbĭmŭs |

## OF FEET CALLED ISOCHRONOUS.

1. Feet that are in metre, considered interchangeable or convertible, have been called *Isochronous*.\* For instance, as a *long* syllable contains *two times*, while a *short* syllable contains but *one time*, the Spondee consisting of two long syllables is *Isochronous*, or of equal-time, with the Anapæst consisting of two short and one long;—with the Dactyl consisting of one long and two short;—or with the Proceleusmatic consisting of four short syllables: and *vice versa*: as in the following scheme:—

| The Spondee        | — \| —           |
|--------------------|------------------|
| The Anapæst        | ⌣ ⌣ \| —         |
| The Dactyl         | — \| ⌣ ⌣         |
| The Proceleusmatic | ⌣ ⌣ \| ⌣ ⌣       |

thus the long or double time of the first member or first half of the Spondee, is equivalent to, or convertible into the two single times of the Anapæst, while the double time of the second member or second half, is equivalent to, or convertible into, the two single times of the Dactyl:—and the double time of either member of the Spondee, answers a similar purpose for either half of the Proceleusmatic: and so again the times of each of the three, are resolvable into those of the Spondee.† But of the other feet, the Iambus is not substituteable for the Trochee; nor is the Spondee for the Amphibrach.

---

\* That is, *even* or *equal-timed;* from ἴσος, "equal," and χρόνος, "time."

† The young Prosodian must beware of misconception on this subject; because, critically speaking, no feet are Isochronous, unless they are so in their *separate* members, as the four above compared; whose first and second members consist of equal times. Therefore neither a Trochee nor an Amphibrach is Isochronous with any of the four just mentioned. Of this any one may be convinced by pronouncing the words rĕclūdĕ, rĕsūmĕ, rĕpĕllĕ,—three Amphibrachic feet—and comparing them with three Dactyls, ēlŭdĕrĕ, sūmĕrĕ, pēllĕrĕ; the voice requiring more time for the distinct enunciation of the three former than of the three latter; because the voice dwells longer on each of the short syllables when separate, than when following each other consecutively.

2. The *arsis** is naturally assigned to the long syllable of every foot: in the iambus to the second syllable; in the trochee to the first, while on the spondee and tribrach, the position of the *arsis* must depend on circumstances: because as the predominant foot and metre always determine the position for the subordinate feet, the spondee when intoduced into iambic or anapæstic verse, has the *arsis* on the *second* syllable, but in trochaic or dactylic verse on the *first:* so the tribra$_{\text{ch}}$ introduced in iambic verse, has the *arsis* on the *third*, and when in trochaic, on the *first*.

## SECTION VII.

### OF METRE.

1. METRE is most commonly used to signify a combination of verses succeeding each other in regular order: thus *Dactylic metre*, *Iambic metre*, *Trochaic metre*, are synonymous with *Dactylic*, *Iambic*, *Trochaic verse*.

2. METRE is also used in a more restricted sense to signify either a single foot or a combination of feet in poetry, and in this sense, it is technically called " *a metre.*"

3. The metres employed in Latin poetry, are six: viz.,—1. the *Dactylic;* 2. the *Anapæstic;* 3. the *Iambic;* 4. the *Trochaic;* 5. the *Choriambic;* 6. the *Ionic:*† to which may be added another, irreducible to any of these six, under the head of *Compound Verses*, as the 7th kind.

---

* See pp. 2, 74, and 81, for an account of the *arsis*.
† These metres are thus designated from their predominance in some particular foot; as each species had been originally composed of those feet only, whence the name was given: but other feet of equal time, were afterwards occasionally substituted, according as the taste of the poet or the necessity of the verse required. Metres are not unfrequently denominated after some celebrated poet who composed in this particular species: as the *Alcaic*, the *Anacreontic*, the *Sapphic*, &c., &c.

4. Metres are likewise divided into eight classes, corresponding to the number of feet or measures which they contain ;. thus, a verse of *eight* metres or feet, is called *Octameter ;*—a verse of *seven* metres is called *Heptameter ;*—a verse of *six*, *Hexameter ;*—a verse of *five*, *Pentameter ;*—of four, *Tetrameter ;*—of *three*, *Trimeter ;*—of *two*, *Dimeter ;*—of *one*, *Monometer*.

5. In *Dactylic*, *Choriambic*, and *Ionic* verse, a *metre* consists of *one* foot only ; but in *Anapæstic*, *Iambic*, and *Trochaic* verse, *a metre* contains *two* feet ;—thus, in the three former, a *Monometer* consists of *one* foot ;—a *Dimeter*, of *two* feet ;—a *Trimeter*, of *three* ;—a *Tetrameter*, of *four* :—a *Pentameter*, of *five* ;—an *Hexameter*, of *six* ; and an *Heptameter*, of *seven* feet, while in the three latter, a *Monometer* contains two feet ;—a *Dimeter* contains *four* feet ;—a *Trimeter*, *six* ;—a *Tetrameter*, *eight* ;—a *Pentameter*, *ten* ;—an *Hexameter*, *twelve* ;—and an *Heptameter*, *fourteen.*\*

6. SCANNING† is the technical division of a line or verse into its component feet. It also assigns to each of these component feet its proper quantity.

DIRECTIONS FOR SCANNING. A vowel, or a diphthong, or a syllable composed of a vowel and *M*, is cut off from the end of a word, when the next word begins with a vowel. This is called *Elision*. Thus,

Quidve moror? si omnes uno ordine habetis Achivos. *Vir.*
Gentis Iuleæ, et rapti secreta Quirini. *Lucan.*
Monstrum horrendum, informe, ingens, cui lumen ademtum.
*Virg.*

---

\* Two consecutive feet are sometimes called a *dipodia*, (διποδία) or *Syzygy*, (συζυγία): in general, however, two dissyllabic feet are termed a *dipodia*, while two trisyllabic feet, or a dissyllabic and trisyllabic together, is called a *syzygy*. The combination of two feet is also called a *base*.

‡ Or "Scanding" from *Scandere*, "to climb"; as if mounting, climbing, or advancing through the poem, step by step. Among the polished nations of antiquity, more attention was paid to scanning, as indispensable to the elegant reading of verse, than among the moderns; who do not seem conscious of the poet's rebuke—

Scandere qui nescis, versiculos laceras.

must be read in scanning

> Quidve moror? s' omnes un' ordin' habetis Achivos.
> Gentis Iule', et rapti secreta Quirini
> Monstr' horrend', inform', ingens, cui lumen ademtum.

The elision of a vowel or diphthong is called *Synalœpha;* that of *m* and the vowel before it, *Ecthlipsis.* The earlier poets frequently elided *s* final before a consonant, to preserve the vowel from becoming long by position; as,

> ... Sive foras fertur, non est ea *fini'* profecto.   *Lucret.*
> Sceptra potitus, eadem aliis *sopitu'* quiete est     *Id.*

And when the next word begins with a vowel, the *s* is sometimes cut off to expose the vowel before it to Elision; as,

> Etenim ille *quoiu' huc* jussu venio Jupiter [Iambic Trim.]
>                                                  *Plautus.*

To be sounded " *quo' huc.*" And in Lucretius, III. 1048, we ought to read

> Ossa dedit terræ, proinde ac *famulu'* infimus esset.

instead of *famul,* as it is commonly printed.

*Exc.* The interjections *o, heu, ah, proh,* never suffer elision.

7. Verses are called *Acatalectic,*\* *Catalectic,*† *Brachycatalectic, Hypercatalectic,* (or *Hypermeter,*) and *Acephalous.*‡ A line or verse that contains an exact number of feet without deficiency or excess, is called *Acatalectic;* a line or verse that wants *one* syllable of a certain regular number of feet, is called *Catalectic,* or *deficient by one;* a verse wanting *two,* is called *Brachycatalectic,* or *deficient*

---

\* From ἀκαταληκτικός, (fr. *a priv.* and καταλήγω, "I stop, or cease.")
† From καταληκτικός, denoting verses that stop short before completion; wanting one syllable. Hence the derivation of the next two kinds is evident.
‡ From ἀκέφαλος. (fr. *a priv.* and κεφαλή, "head") without a head.

*by two;* and if a verse have one or two syllables superfluous, after the regular number of feet is complete, it is called *Hypercatalectic* or *Hypermeter;* i. e., *redundant;* while a verse that wants a syllable at the beginning, is called *Acephalous* or *headless.*

### COMBINATIONS OF VERSE.

A poem written in stanzas of { two / three / four / five } lines is called { *Distrŏphos\** or *Distrŏphon.* / *Tristrŏphos* or *Tristrŏphon.* / *Tetrastrŏphos* or *Tetrastrŏphon.* / *Pentastrŏphos* or *Pentastrŏphon.* }

A poem written in { one kind / two kinds / three kinds } of verse is called { *Monocŏlos†* or *Monocŏlon.* / *Dicŏlos* or *Dicŏlon.* / *Tricŏlos* or *Tricŏlon.* }

Hence poetic composition is distinguished and denominated after two different ways; viz.—1st, according to the variety [or kinds] of verse used;—2dly, from the number of verses, of which it consists, previous to the completion of each strophe; *i. e.*, before the poem *returns* to the same kind of verse, with which it had commenced.

First, according to the variety [or kinds] of verse used: —a poem written in one kind or sort of verse, is called *Monocŏlos,* or *Monocŏlon;*‡ a poem written in two kinds or sorts of verse, is called *Dicŏlos,* or *Dicŏlon;*§ a poem written in three kinds or sorts of verse, is called *Tricŏlos,* or *Tricŏlon.*‖

Secondly, according to the number of verses in each strophe. When the same kind of verse with which a poem commenced, recurs after the *second* line, the poem is denominated *Distrŏphos* or *Distrŏphon;*¶ when the same kind of verse recurs after the *third* line, the poem

---

\* From δις, "twice or double," and στροφή, "a stanza:" and so of the rest.

† From μόνος, "single," and κῶλον, "a member;"—and so of the others.

‡ As the Eclogues, Georgics, and Æneis of Virgil, the Satires of Horace, and Ovid's Metamorphosis,—all consisting of hexameters.

§ As Ovid's Epistles, the Elegies of Tibullus, &c., &c., composed in hexameters and pentameters alternately.

‖ As the Alcaics of Horace.

¶ As iii. Ode, Lib. i. of Horace.

is denominated *Tristrŏphos* or *Tristrŏphon;* * when the same kind recurs after the *fourth* line, it is denominated *Tetrastrŏphos* or *Tetrastrŏphon;*† and so of the rest.

Then by a combination of the preceding terms, a poem written in stanzas, consisting of *two* verses of different kinds, is called *Dicōlon-Distrŏphon;*‡ when the stanza consists of three verses, but of two sorts only, (one sort being twice repeated,) it is called *Dicōlon-tristrŏphon;*§ when the stanza consists of four verses,—still of two sorts only, (one being thrice repeated,) it is called *Dicōlon-tetrastrŏphon.*‖ When the poem is written in stanzas consisting of three lines, each of a different kind, it is called *Tricōlon-tristrŏphon;*¶ when a stanza consists of *four* verses, but of three kinds only, (one being repeated,) it is called *Tricŏlon-tetrastrŏphon;*** and so of the rest.

## SECTION VIII.

### DIFFERENT KINDS OF VERSE.

#### GENUS I. DACTYLIC VERSES.

1. *General Canon.* These have their last foot always a spondee,†† and the last but one always a dactyl, while the rest may indiscriminately be either dactyles or spondees. The penultimate foot is very seldom a spondee, but when it is so, a dactyl most generally precedes it.

2. SPECIES 1.—*Dactylic Hexameter* or *Heroic Verse*

---

* As Ode xi. lib. Epod. of Horace, and the Preface to the Hymns of Prudentius.
† As Ode ii. lib. i. of Horace.
‡ As the Elegiacs of Ovid, Catullus, Propertius, Tibullus, and many of Horace's Odes.
§ As Ode xii. lib. iii. of Horace.
‖ As Ode ii. lib. i. of Horace, already quoted.
¶ As Ode xi. and xiii. lib. Epod. of Horace.
** As Ode ix. lib. i. of Horace.
†† Because a dactyl at the end, would become an amphimacer.

consists of six feet,* varied and limited as above: i. e., five dactyls and one spondee; admitting a spondee instead of a dactyl, on any of the first four places, but on the fifth, rarely: according to the following scale—

| 1 | 2 | 3 | 4 | 5 | 6 |
|---|---|---|---|---|---|
| —⏑⏑ | —⏑⏑ | —⏑⏑ | —⏑⏑ | —⏑⏑ | —— |
| —— | —— | —— | —— |   |   |

Rădĭtĭ\|tēr lĭquĭ\|dūm, cĕlĕ-\|rēs nĕquĕ \| cōmmŏvĕt\|ālās. *Vir.*
ōllī \| rēspōn\|dĭt rēx \| Ālbā\|ī lōn\|gāī. *Ennius.*
Lūdĕrĕ \| quæ vĕl-\|lĕm călă-\|mō pēr-\|mīsĭt ă\|grēstī. *Vrg.*
Mārgĭnĕ \| tērrā-\|rŭm pōr-\|rēxĕrăt \| Āmphī-\|trītē. *Ovid.*

The fifth foot should never be a spondee, unless for the purpose of expressing slow or difficult motion, in solemn, majestic, or mournful descriptions, or in those expressive of dignity, gravity, astonishment, consternation, vastness of extent, &c., &c.

3. SPECIES 2.—*Dactylic Tetrameter a priore* consists of the first four feet of the ordinary hexameter varied and limited as in Art. 1; with this difference, that the fourth or last foot is always a dactyl.

Lūmĭnĭ-\|bŭs quĕ prī-\|ōr rĕdĭ-\|ĭt vĭgŏr.   *Boethius.*
Gārrŭlă \| pēr rā-\|mōs ăvĭs \| ōbstrĕpĭt.   *Seneca.*

4. SPECIES 3.—*Dactylic Tetrameter a posteriore*, has the last four feet of an hexameter; as,

---

* As each of these feet—whether dactyls or spondees—contains four times, there are consequently in every line or verse—prosodially speaking—twenty-four times. So also in every other species of verse, must the number of times, in proportion to the number of its feet, be inviolably preserved. Hence appears the absurdity of attempting to read Latin verse, according to the rules of English accent and quantity; by which the twenty-four times of an hexameter line are often extended to twenty-nine times!!—not unfrequently to thirty-one!!! ☞ It may be useful to the young Prosodian to bear in mind, that every regular Hexameter verse or line must contain not fewer than *thirteen*, and not more than *seventeen*, syllables; i. e., the line or verse may consist of five spondees and one dactyl (the penultimate foot), making thirteen syllables; or of five dactyls and one spondee, making seventeen syllables.

Ībĭmŭs\|ō sŏcĭ-\|ī cŏmĭ-\|tēsque. *Hor.*
Jūdĭcĕ\|tē nōn\|sōr dĭdŭs\|aūctōr. *Idem.*
Mēnsō-\|rēm cōhĭ-\|bēnt Ār-\|chȳtā. *Idem.*

5. SPECIES 4.—*Tetrameter Catalectic* is the last species with its final syllable cut off; as,

Ībĭmŭs\|ō sŏcĭ-\|ī cŏmĭ-\|tēs.
Ūnŭs ĕ-\|nīm rē-\|rūm pătĕr\|ēst. *Boëth.*

6. SPECIES 5.—*Trimeter (Pherecratic)* consists of a spondee, a dactyl, and a spondee without variation; as,

Crās dō-\|nābĕrĭs\|hædō. *Hor.*

\*\*\* By some *P*rosodians this is scanned as a choriambic. See Art. 34, under that head.

7. SPECIES 6.—*Trimeter Catalectic (Archilochian)* consists of two dactyls and a syllable; a spondee being seldom admitted; as,

Ārbŏrĭ-\|būsque cŏ-\|mæ. *Hor.*

8. SPECIES 7.—*Dimeter (Adonic\*)* consists of a dactyl and a spondee without variation; as,

Tērrŭĭt\|ūrbēm. *Hor.*

The *Adonic* is rarely used unless joined to the Trochaic, *P*entameter or Sapphic: one *Adonic* being annexed to three Sapphics, to form the strophe or stanza. In tragic choruses, however, it is annexed to any number of Sapphics at the will of the poet.†

IRREGULAR DACTYLIC VERSES.‡

*Of Pentameter.*

9. SPECIES 1.—*Pentameter* consists of five feet, of

---

\*. So called from the metre used in lamenting the fate of Adonis.
† See *Seneca, Œdip.* act 1;—*Troas*, act 4;—*Herc. Fur.* act 3;—*Thyest.* act 3, &c.
‡ Those verses are called irregular, because they deviate from the general canon laid down at the beginning of the genus.

which the first and second are either dactyls or spondees, the third is always a spondee, and the fourth and fifth are anapæsts, according to the scale—

| 1 | 2 | 3 | 4 | 5 |
|---|---|---|---|---|
| — ◡ ◡ | — ◡ ◡ | — — | ◡ ◡ — | ◡ ◡ — |

Lāssā-|rēt vĭdŭ-|ās pēn-|dŭlă tē-|lă mănūs. *Ovid.*
Ĕt grăcī-|lĭs strŭc-|tōs ēf-|fŭgīt ūm-|brā rŏgōs. *Idem.*

The *Pentameter* must always have a cæsura *Penthemimeris*; and every line ought to conclude with a dissyllable; as a trisyllable is considered inelegant.

Another mode of dividing the *Pentameter*, and which is preferred by the best *Prosodians*,—is to separate each line into two Catalectic Trimeters (7), the first admitting the spondee, the second not: in other words, the first two feet may be either dactyls or spondees, followed by a long syllable, then two dactyls followed by another long syllable: according to the scale—

| 1 | 2 | 3 | 4 | 5 | 6 |
|---|---|---|---|---|---|
| — ◡ ◡ | — ◡ ◡ | — | — ◡ ◡ | — ◡ ◡ | — |

Lāssā-|rēt vĭdŭ-|ās‖pēndŭlă|tēlă mă-|nūs.
Ĕt grăcī-|lĭs strŭc-|tōs‖ēffŭgĭt|ūmbrā rŏ-|gōs.

10. SPECIES 2.—*Alcmanian Tetrameter Hypercatalectic** consists of two divisions, the first being a dactylic

---

* Carey who has been followed by Anthon and other distinguished classical scholars—calls it *Phalæcian*, on the authority, it is alleged, of Terentianus. But this writer's meaning appears to have been misunderstood on this passage. Terentianus in describing that particular form of verse in the above text, remarks, that it is *hendecasyllabic*. But as in making this remark, he *uses* a *Phalæcian* verse, to which species, the term *hendecasyllabic* is almost exclusively confined. he adds, in his prolix manner, that the verse he is describing is *alter*—"differ-

penthemimeris, *i. e.*, two feet and a half from the beginning of an Hexameter, and the second a dactyl and spondee; as,

Heū quām|prǣcĭpĭ-|tĭ||mērsă prŏ-|fŭndō.  *Boëthius.*

This might be scanned as a common *P*entameter deficient by a semifoot; as,

Hēu quām|prǣcĭpĭ-|tĭ mēr-|să prŏfŭn-|dō.

or still again as a Choriambic Catalectic Tetrameter; as,

Hēu quām|prǣcĭpĭtĭ|mērsă prŏfŭn|dō.

### GENUS II. ANAPÆSTIC VERSES.

**11.** *General Canon.* The Anapæst is everywhere convertible into a dactyl or a spondee, [and sometimes into a proceleusmatic] with this limitation, that a dactyl is rarely found in an even place: *i. e.*, in the second or fourth;—according to the following scale of the Anapæstic Dimeter—

| 1 | 2 | 3 | 4 |
|---|---|---|---|
| ⏑ ⏑ — | ⏑ ⏑ — | ⏑ ⏑ — | ⏑ ⏑ — |
| — — | — — | — — | — — |
| — ⏑ ⏑ | — ⏑ ⏑ | — ⏑ ⏑ | — ⏑ ⏑ |

**12.** Species 1.—*The Anapæstic series* is not limited to any definite number of feet, but runs on *continuo carmine*, till it stops short at a pause in the sense, sometimes in the middle of a foot. It then begins again, runs on and stops short as before; and so on to the end of the poem. It is sometimes printed in verses of four feet; as,

Īndūs|gĕlĭdūm||pōtăt Ār-|āxēm,
Ālbīm|Pērsǣ,||Rhēnūm-|quē bĭbūnt.

ent,"—from that he is using;—"for the latter," says he, "is *Phalæcian*, which shall be *afterwards* described." In the original his words are—

Fiet hendecasyllabos, sed alter,
Namque hic de genere est Phalæciorum,
Cujus mox tibi regulam loquemur.

Vĕnĭent|ānnĭs||sæcŭlă|sĕrīs;
Quĭbŭs Ō|cĕānŭs||vīncŭlă|rērŭm,
Lāxĕt ĕt|īngēns||pătĕāt|tēllūs
Tīphȳs-|quĕ nŏvōs||dētĕgăt|ōrbēs.
Nēc sīt|tērrĭs||ūltĭmă|Thūlē.* *Seneca.*

Sometimes in verses of two feet; as,

Dēflē | tĕ vĭrūm,
Quō nōn | ălĭūs
Pŏtŭīt | cĭtĭūs
Dīscĕrĕ caūsās. *Seneca.*

But divide them as we may in printing, we should always *scan* the whole paragraph as one line, the verses being connected by Synapheia,† and a short syllable at the end of a line being always lengthened by a consonant or consonants at the beginning of the next: as the final syllables of *virŭm,*‡ *alĭŭs, citĭŭs,* in the above examples.

13. Species 2.—*Anapæstic Tetrameter Catalectic* (or, as called by others, *Dimeter Catalectic* or *Parœmiac*) consists of three anapæsts and a syllable; varied by the admission of a spondee on the first two places; as,

Nēc vīnct-|tă lĭbī-|dĭnĕ cōl-|lā.
Fœdīs | sūbmīt-|tăt hăbē-|nīs. *Boëth.*

GENUS III. IAMBIC VERSES.

14. *General Canon.* Iambic verse is of two kinds, pure and mixed. The pure admits no foot except the iambus; the mixed admits spondees on the odd places—the first, third, &c., and allows any long syllable to be

---

* This remarkable prophecy uttered nearly 1500 years before its accomplishment, has been verified to an extraordinary degree, by the discovery of America, and its colonization from Europe. The poet doubtless drew his inspiration from some of the Sybilline vaticinations extant in his day.
† See *Synapheia,* p. 78.
‡ *M* litera terminatus accusativus, in omni genere semper brevem habet. *Val. Probus,* i. See also Servius *de ultimis syllabis;* and Diomedes, iii.

resolved into two short, by which means, an iambus may be converted into a tribrach, and a spondee into a dactyl, an anapæst, or a proceleusmatic. Iambic verse, then, admits on the even places a tribrach, and on the odd, a tribrach, a spondee, dactyl, anapæst or a proceleusmatic. But a tribrach is never admitted into the last place, nor a proceleusmatic into any but the first;* according to the following scale of an *Iambic Trimeter Acatalectic.*

| 1 | 2 | 3 | 4 | 5 | 6 |
|---|---|---|---|---|---|
| ᴗ — | | ᴗ — | ᴗ — | ᴗ — | ᴗ — |
| ᴗ ᴗ ᴗ | ᴗ ᴗ ᴗ | ᴗ ᴗ ᴗ | ᴗ ᴗ ᴗ | ᴗ ᴗ ᴗ | |
| — — | | — — | | — — | |
| ᴗ ᴗ — | | ᴗ ᴗ — | | ᴗ ᴗ — | |
| — ᴗ ᴗ | | — ᴗ ᴗ | | — ᴗ ᴗ | |
| ᴗ ᴗ ᴗ ᴗ | | | | | |

15. Species 1.—*Iambic Tetrameter* or *Octonarius* consists of eight feet, that is, four metres or measures; and admits all the variations; as,

*Pure.* Ădēst|cĕlēr||phăsē|lŭs ĭl||lĕ quēm|vĭdē||tĭs hōs|pītēs.
*Catullus.*

*Mixed.* Sānē|pŏl ĭs||tă tē|mŭlēn||ta ēst mŭlĭ|ĕr ēt||tĕmĕrā|rĭā.
*Terence.*

And agreeably to the practice of the comic poets:—

Ātque ēst|hæc ĕă||dēm quæ|mĭhī dīx||tī tŭ|tē dī||cās mŭlĭ|ĕrī.
*Idem.*

16· Species 2.—*Tetrameter Catalectic* consists of seven iambics and a syllable, admitting the variations; as,

*Pure.* Rĕmīt|tĕ pāl||lĭūm|mĭhī||mĕūm|quŏd īn||vŏlās|tī.
*Catullus.*

---

* Writers of Comedy and of Fable (the latter more sparingly), that their language might approach nearer to that of common life, admit the spondee and its equivalents into all the even places but the last.

*Mixed.* Quūm dēͥvĭā‖mŭlĭĕr|ăvēs‖ōstēn|dĭt ōs‖cĭtān|tēs.
*Idem.*

And according to the comic license ;—

Nōn pōs|sūm sătĭ'|nārrā|rĕ quōs‖lūdōs|præbŭĕ‖rĭs īn|tūs.
*Terence.*

**17. Species 3.**—*Trimeter* or *Senarius* (as in the above scale) consists of six feet with all the variations; as,

*Pure.* Sŭīs|ĕt īp‖sā Rō|mā vī‖rĭbūs|rŭīt.    *Hor.*

*Mixed.* { Ālĭtĭ|bŭs āt‖qŭe cănĭ|bŭs hŏmĭ‖cīdam Hĕc|tŏrā.
*Idem.*
Rēx, ād|vŏcā‖tā cōn|cĭō-ne,|hæc ē|dĭdĭt. *Phæd.*

And by the usage of comedy and fable :—

Īnfēs-|tīs Tāu-‖rūs mōx-|cōnfō-‖dĭt cōr-|nĭbūs. *Phædrus.*
Jām mūl-|tōs ān-‖nōs ēst,|cūm pōs‖sĭdĕo ĕt-|cŏlō. *Plau.*

**18. Species 4.**—*Trimeter Catalectic* consists of five feet and a syllable. It admits the variations, except that the spondee is rarely if ever admitted into the fifth place, but is into the first and third ; as,

*Pure.* Pīūs|fīdē-‖līs īn-|nŏcēns‖pŭdī-|cŭs.  *Prudentius.*
*Mixed.* Rēgūm|qŭe pŭĕ-‖rīs ; nēc|sătēl-‖lĕs ōr-|cī. *Hor.*

**19. Species 5.**—*Dimeter Hypermeter* consists of four feet and a syllable, admitting the spondee on the odd places; as,

Nōn vūl-|tūs īn-‖stāntīs|tўrān-‖nī.    *Horace.*

**20. Species 6.**—*Dimeter* or *Quaternarius* has four feet, admitting the variations ;—

*Pure.* Săcēr|nĕpō-‖tĭbūs|crŭōr.    *Horace.*
*Mixed.* Mĕrītīs|rĕpēn-‖dĕt cōn-|grŭā. *Prudentius.*

Most of the beautiful hymns in the *Roman Breviary*

DIFFERENT KINDS OF VERSE.   101

and in the public service of the Catholic Church, are composed in this metre; such as that exquisite Morning Hymn—

>     Jām lū|cĭs ōr-‖tō sī|dĕrē, &c., &c.,—
> or ...... Jēsū|cŏrō-‖nă vīr-|gĭnūm, &c., &c.,—
> or again .. Vēxīl-|lă rē-‖gĭs prō-|dĕūnt, &c., &c.,—

all three justly attributed to St. Ambrose: although the last has been assigned to Venantius Honorius Fortunatus.*

In these Dimeters, we find, that, with few exceptions, strict attention has been paid to the rules of Prosody; the verses generally terminating with a trisyllable, which is their best cadence.† Some of these hymns, however excellent in piety and elevated sentiment, are very indifferent specimens of Prosodial composition; as—

>     Jēsū,|nōstră‖rĕdēm-|tĭō, &c.,

* A more beautiful or a more comprehensive matutinal prayer can scarcely be offered his Creator by the pious student of any religious denomination, than the first of the foregoing hymns. We are therefore induced to give it entire for the reminiscence of the youthful reader: remarking, that, in reading or recitation, the judicious Prosodian anxious to preserve its harmony and melody, will cause the *ictus metricus* to fall, *Iambico more*, on every alternate syllable: as thus marked—

> Jām lú|cĭs ór‖tō sí|dĕré,
> Deum precemur supplices,
> Ut in diurnis actibus
> Nos servet a nocentibus.
> Linguam refrænans temperet,
> Ne litis horror insonet.
> Visum fovendo contegat,
> Ne vanitates hauriat.
> Sint pura cordis intima;
> Absistat et vecordia.
> Carnis terat superbiam
> Potûs cibique parcitas:
> Ut cum dies abscesserit,
> Noctemque sors reduxerit,
> Mundi per abstinentiam
> Ipsi canamus gloriam:
> Deo Patri sit gloria,
> Ejusque soli Filio,
> Cûm Spiritu Paracleto,
> Nunc, et per omne seculum.

† Much of the sweetness, delicacy and *curiosa felicitas* of these chaste effusions of the Christian Muse, is undoubtedly lost to the readers of Latin Hymns, unacquainted with Prosody.

and could never have emanated from the classic pen of the accomplished St. Ambrose; to whom this also has been attributed.

21. Species 7. *Dimeter Catalectic* or *Anacreontic* consists of three feet and a syllable. It admits in the first position, a tribrach, a spondee, or an amphibrach; rarely allowing a spondee in the third; as—

Pure. { Lēx hæc|dăta ēst‖cădū-|cīs,
        Dĕō|jŭbēn-‖tē, mēm-|brīs;
Mixed. { Ūt tēm-|pĕrēt‖lăbō-|rēm,
         Mĕdĭcā-|bĭlīs‖vŏlūp-|tās.                    *Prudentius.*

IRREGULAR IAMBIC VERSES.

22. Species 1.—*Galliambus*\* is composed of two Anacreontics (21), with the final syllable cut off: that is, an Anacreontic followed by three feet. The third foot of both members is always an iambus, and the last but one of the whole is commonly a tribrach; as in the scale following—

| 1 | 2 | 3 | 4 | 5 | 6 | 7 |
|---|---|---|---|---|---|---|
| ⏑⏑⎯ / ⎯⎯ / ⏑⏑⏑ | ⏑⏑⏑ | ⏑⎯ | ⎯ | ⎯⎯ / ⏑⏑⎯ | ⏑⎯ / ⏑⏑⏑ | ⏑⎯ |

Jām jām|dŏlēt‖quŏd ē-|gī,‖jām jām-|quĕ pǣ-‖nĭtēt. *Catul.*
Rŏsēīs|ŭt huīc‖lăbĕl-|lĭs‖pălāns|sŏnĭtŭs‖ăbīt.        *Idem.*
Ĕgŏ mŭlī-|ĕr ĕgŏ ăd-‖ŏlēs-|cēns,‖ĕgŏ ĕphē|bŭs, ĕgŏ‖pŭēr.
                                                      *Idem.*

Some *Prosodians* mark the scale and divide the lines differently; but the scale and metre above are in accordance with the structure of the only specimen of the Galliambus extant,—Catullus's Atys; in which the tribrach in the penultimate foot is predominant.

\* So called from its use by the *Galli*, or priests of Cybele, in their **orgies.**

23. SPECIES 2.*—The *Scazon* or *Choriambus* has six feet; the sixth always a spondee, the fifth always an iambus, and the rest varied as in Art. 14; thus—

Mīsĕr|Cătūl-‖lĕ dē-|sĭnās‖ĭnēp-|tīrē. *Catull.*
Pĭĕtā-|tĕ frā-‖trēs Cū-|rĭōs‖lĭcēt|vīncās. *Martial.*

24. SPECIES 3.—*Iambic Alcaic*, commonly called *Greater Alcaic*, consists of five feet, of which the fourth is always an anapæst, and the rest are iambuses, admitting the spondee on the first and third; but as in the *Dimeter Hypermeter*, (19), the first foot is seldom an iambus, the third scarcely ever; as—

Vīrtūs|rĕpūl-‖sæ nēs-|cĭă sōr-|dĭdæ. *Horace.*

The *Greater Alcaic* is sometimes scanned with a choriambus and an iambus, in the latter member or colon; as—

Vīrtūs|rĕpūl-|sæ‖nēscĭă sōr-|dĭdæ.

The *Alcaic* is also scanned so as to make the first colon, an iambic measure and a long syllable, and the second, two dactyls: and indeed this is the mode generally followed; as—

Vīrtūs|rĕpūl|sæ‖nēscĭă | sōrdĭdæ.†

GENUS IV. TROCHAIC VERSES.

25. *General Canon.* The trochee is everywhere convertible into a tribrach; the same feet are also admitted into the even places, that iambic verse receives into the odd.

26. SPECIES 1.—*Trochaic Tetrameter Catalectic* con-

---

* Although the *Saturnian* ought, in regular order, find a place here, as species 2, still it has not been deemed requisite to introduce it, from its manifest inutility to the young Prosodian.
† This affords an example of the *poëtica licentia* in closing the line with a long syllable, although the measure requires a short one. See p. 49, *supra*.

sists of seven feet and a syllable. A tribrach is rarely admitted into the sixth place, never into the seventh, except in some few passages in comedy. In the case of proper names, a dactyl is admissible into any place but the fourth and seventh; as in the following scale—

| 1 | 2 | 3 | 4 | 5 | 6 | 7 |
|---|---|---|---|---|---|---|
| −⏑ | −⏑ | −⏑ | −⏑ | −⏑ | −⏑ | −⏑ − |
| ⏑⏑⏑ | ⏑⏑⏑ | ⏑⏑⏑ | ⏑⏑⏑ | ⏑⏑⏑ | ⏑⏑⏑ | |
| | − − | − − | | − − | − − | |
| | −⏑⏑ | | −⏑⏑ | | −⏑⏑ | |
| | ⏑⏑− | | ⏑⏑− | | ⏑⏑− | |
| proper name −⏑⏑ | −⏑⏑ | −⏑⏑ | | −⏑⏑ | −⏑⏑ | |

*Pure.* Tē sŏ-|cēr sŭb-‖īrĕ|cēlsă‖pōscĭt|āstră‖jūpĭ-|tēr.
*Mart. Capella.*

*Mixed.* Īmpĭ-|ūm răpĭ-‖te, ātquĕ|mērsūm‖prĕmītĕ|pērpĕtŭ-‖īs mā-|līs.
*Seneca.*

The comic writers, although scarcely venturing to alter the seventh foot, introduce the spondee and its equivalents into the odd places; by a license similar to that employed in iambic verse; as,

Quēm rēs|ætās‖ūsūs|sēmpĕr‖ălĭquĭd|āppōr-‖tēt nŏ|vī.
*Terence.*

In this metre also are written many of the Latin hymns used in the Catholic Church; for which purpose it is admirably adapted from its grand, solemn, and sonorous character: such as that noble hymn on the *Passion* of our Lord—

Pāngĕ,|līngŭa,‖glōrĭ-|ōsī‖laūrĕ-|ām cēr-‖tămĭn-|īs.
*St. Augustinus.*

This is undoubtedly the true mode of writing and scanning this beautiful poem, making every stanza consist of three lines or verses; contrary to the mode usually followed in the Roman Breviary, of dividing each line

## DIFFERENT KINDS OF VERSE. 105

into two hemistichs: the first a Trochaic Dimeter, and the other a Trochaic Dimeter Catalectic; by which every stanza consists of six lines; thus,

Pāngĕ,‖līngŭa‖glōrĭ-|ōsĭ,‖
Laūrĕ-|ām cēr-‖tāmĭn-|īs.

This division, although contrary to all *P*rosodial rules, was made to suit the convenience of the choir;—one side —or perhaps one choir—singing the complete dimeter, and the other the dimeter Catalectic. Some *P*rosodians scan this verse as an *Iambic Tetrameter Acephalous;* as,

—Pān-|gĕ līn‖guă glō-|rĭō‖sī laū-|rĕām‖cērtā-|mĭnīs:—

but with a manifest diminution of its stately movement and sonorous majesty. It is worthy of remark, that many hymns in this metre can be read with a strict observance of modern accentuation without violating the Latin quantity; as,

Sólve vócem, méns, sonóram;‖sólve línguam móbilem.
*Prudentius.*
Scánde cǽli témpla, vírgo,‖dígna tánto fœ́dere.*
*M. Capella.*

27 SPECIES 2.—*Dimeter Catalectic (Euripedean)* consists of three trochees and a syllable without variation; as,

Lārgĭ|ōră‖flāgĭ-|tō. *Hor.*
Dōnă|cōnscĭ-‖ēntĭ-|æ. *Prudent.*

### IRREGULAR TROCHAIC VERSES.

28. SPECIES 1.—*Sapphic*† consists of a dactyl inserted

---

* The young Prosodian should observe, that in all these hymns, the cæsura uniformly takes place at the termination of the fourth foot, corresponding with the fifth semifoot of the Iambic trimeter: hence too, in a great measure, sprung the error of the copyists and editors of the Breviary in dividing the verses as above mentioned.

† So called from the gifted but ill-starred poetess, its inventor

between two trochaic measures; or in other words, of five feet, viz., a trochee, a spondee, a dactyl and two more trochees; followed by an *Adonic* or *Dactylic Dimeter* (8); according to the following scale:

|   | 1 | 2 | 3 | 4 | 5 |
|---|---|---|---|---|---|
|   | — ᴗ | — — | — ᴗ ᴗ | — ᴗ | — ᴗ |
|   | — ᴗ | — — | — ᴗ ᴗ | — ᴗ | — ᴗ |
|   | — ᴗ | — — | — ᴗ ᴗ | — ᴗ | — ᴗ |
| *Adonic.* |   |   |   | — ᴗ ᴗ | — — |

Īntĕ-|gēr vī-|tæ,* scĕlĕ-|rīsquĕ|pūrŭs.
Nōn ĕ-|gēt Māu-|rī* jăcŭ-|līs nĕc|ārcŭ.*
Nēc vĕ-|nēnā-|tīs* grăvī-|dā să-|gīttĭs,
  Fūscĕ, phă-|rētrā. *Hor.*

An iambus, a trochee or a dactyl is sometimes admitted into the second place; but with Horace it is invariably a spondee; and the great Roman Lyrist is the safest guide.

The asterisk * marks the *cæsura* after the second foot, or rather the fifth semifoot. In reciting these odes, the pupil should be taught to pay special attention to the cæsura, and the pause thereby required; for in no other position will the sweetness and harmony of this delightful metre be fully preserved.

29. SPECIES 2.—The *Phalæcian*† (sometimes called *Hendecasyllabic*) has five feet, of which the second is a dactyl and the rest trochees: but the first—in violation of the general canon, Art. 25,—is almost always a spondee: so that it may be said to consist of a spondee, a dactyl, and three trochees; as—

  Nōn ēst|vīvĕrĕ,|sēd vă-|lērĕ,|vītă. *Martial.*

---

\* The student must bear in mind what has been stated at p. 49, (note) on the use of a long syllable for a short, and *vice versa*.
† So called from the Poet Phalæcius

This metre is extremely well adapted to the composition of Epigrams. By a slight transposition, the Sapphic may be converted into the Phalæcian; thus the above Sapphic—

*Non eget Mauri jaculis nec arcu,*

may be converted into Phalæcian verse thus—

Nōn Maŭ-|rī jăcŭ-|līs ĕ-|gēt nĕc|ārcŭ.

GENUS V. CHORIAMBIC VERSES.

30. *General Canon.* These have the first foot a trochee, the last an iambus, and the intervening feet choriambuses; that is, they consist of one choriambus or more inserted between the separated members of a choriambus. In some instances, the choriambus is exchanged for an equivalent molossus, and the initial trochee almost always passes into a spondee.

31. SPECIES 1.—*Choriambic Pentameter* (*Choriambic Alcaic*) consists of a spondee, three choriambuses, and an iambus; as,

Nūllām|Vārĕ săcrā|vītĕ prĭūs|sĕvĕrīs ār-|bŏrem. *Hor.*

32. SPECIES 2.—*Tetrameter* (*Asclepiadean*) is the last species with one choriambus omitted; as,

Nūllām|vītĕ prĭūs|sĕvĕrīs ār-|bŏrem.
Mæcē-|nās ătăvīs|ēdĭtĕ rē-|gĭbūs. *Hor.*

As the *cæsura* takes place at the end of the first choriambus, some Prosodians scan this metre as a Dactylic Pentameter, wanting the last syllable; thus,

Mæcē-|nās ătă-|vīs || ēdĭtĕ | rēgĭbūs—

33. SPECIES 3.—*Trimeter* or *Glyconic*\* is the last species with another choriambus thrown out; as,—

\* So called from the poet *Glyco*, its inventor.

Nūllām | ⸺ | ⸺ | sĕvĕrĭs ār-|bŏrēm
Sīc tē | dīvă pŏtēns | Cȳprī.  *Hor.*
Īllī | mōrs grăvĭs īn-|cŭbāt,
Quī nō-|tŭs nĭmĭs ōm-|nĭbūs,
Īgnō-|tŭs mŏrĭtūr | sĭbī.  *Seneca.*

34. SPECIES 4.—*Trimeter Catalectic* or *Pherecratic\** is the *Glyconic* deprived of its final syllable; as,—

Quāmvīs | Pōntĭcă pī-|nūs.  *Horace.*

This may also be considered as the three last feet of an hexameter (6) and thus scanned—

Quāmvīs | Pōntĭcă | pīnūs.

35. SPECIES 5.—A Pherecratic and a Glyconic joined together form what is called *Priapean†  Hexameter;* as,—

Ō cŏ-|lōnĭă qūæ | cŭpīs||pōntĕ | lūdĕrĕ lōn|gō.  *Catullus.*

### IRREGULAR CHORIAMBIC VERSES.

36. SPECIES 1.—*Choriambic Tetrameter Hypermeter* consists of three choriambuses, an iambus and a syllable; (or three choriambuses and a bacchic); as,

Sōlŭs ŏvān|tēm Zĕphȳrŭs | pĕrdŏmĭnē|tŭr ān|nūm.  *Claud.*

Horace has altered the first choriambus to an Epitritus secundus, or *lame* choriambic tetrameter; as—

Tē dĕōs ō-|rō, Sȳbărīn | cūr prŏpĕrēs | ămān-|dō.

37. SPECIES 2.—*Dimeter Hypermeter* (*Aristophanian Choriambic*) consists of a choriambus, an iambus and a syllable; (or of a choriambus and a bacchic;) as,

Lȳdĭă, dīc, | pĕr ōm-|nēs.  *Hor.*

### GENUS VI.  IONIC VERSES.

38. *General Canon.*  Ionic verses are of two kinds, the

---
\* From *Pherecrates.*
† From its use in hymns to Priapus.

Ionic *a majore* and the Ionic *a minore;* or *Ionicus Major* and *Ionicus Minor*:—thus denominated from the feet of which they are respectively composed.

39. Species 1.—*Ionic a minore*, like the Anapæstic (12), is a continued Series, and scanned as one line by Synapheia. If printed in separate verses, the division into tetrameters is to be preferred. *Ionic a minore* is formed as often as may be required, and without variation from the foot whence it derives the name; as—

Mĭsĕrārum ēst | nĕque ămōrī | dărĕ lūdūm, | nĕqŭe dūlcī.
Mălă vīnō | lăvĕre, āut ēx-|ănĭmārī | mĕtŭēntēs.
Pătrŭæ vēr-|bĕră līnguæ, | &c., &c. *Horace.*

40. Species 2.—If from an *Ionic a minore* Tetrameter, the first two syllables are removed, there will remain three *Ionici a majore* and a spondee, forming the *Ionic a majore* or *Sotadic\** verse; as,

——— | Vīnō lăvĕ-|re aūt ēxănī-|mārī mĕtŭ-|ēntēs.

Each of the *Ionici*, particularly the third, is convertible into a ditrochee, and any long syllable may be resolved into two short; as—

Tēr cōrrĭpŭ-|ī tērrĭbī-|lēm mănŭ bĭ-|pēnnēm. *Petronius.*

GENUS VII.  COMPOUND VERSES.

41. Species 1.—*Dactylico-Trochaic Heptameter* (*Archilochian*)—by some called *Logaœdic*† verses—consists of the first four feet of a Dactylic Hexameter, (the fourth being always a dactyl), followed by three trochees; as,

Sōlvĭtŭr | ācrĭs hȳ|ēms grā|tā vĭcĕ||vērĭs|ēt Fā|vōnī. *Hor.*

42. Species 2.—*Dactylic Alcaic*, commonly called

---

\* From *Sotades*, a poet who lampooned Ptolemy Philadelphus in this metre.
‡ From λόγος, "a discourse," and ἀοιδή, "a song," because these verses are a combination of the two metres, viz., trochaic, which approximates ordinary conversation, and of dactylic appropriated to the more elevated soarings of poetry.

*Lesser Alcaic*, consists of two dactyls and a trochaic metre; as,

Flūmĭnă | cōnstĭtĕ-|rīnt ă-|cūtŏ. *Hor.*

This, together with two *Greater Alcaics* (24) and one *Iambic Dimeter Hypermeter* (19), constitutes the celebrated *Alcaic Stanza* of Horace; and to which he was so partial as to compose no fewer than thirty-seven of his exquisite odes, in this metre.

SCALE OF THE ALCAIC STANZA.

*First Two Verses.*

|   | 1 | 2 | 3 | 4 | 5 |
|---|---|---|---|---|---|
|   | ᴗ — | ᴗ — | — | — ᴗ ᴗ | — ᴗ ᴗ |
|   | — — |   |   |   |   |

*Third Verse.*

|   | 1 | 2 | 3 | 4 | 5 |
|---|---|---|---|---|---|
|   | — — | ᴗ — | — — | ᴗ — | — |
|   | ᴗ — |   |   |   |   |

*Fourth Verse.*

|   | 1 | 2 | 3 | 4 |
|---|---|---|---|---|
|   | — ᴗ ᴗ | — ᴗ ᴗ | — ᴗ | — ᴗ |

Ōdī|prŏfā-|nūm||vūlgŭs ĕt|ārcĕŏ :
Fāvē-|tĕ līn|guīs :||cārmĭnă|nōn prĭŭs.
Aūdī-|tă Mū-|sārūm|sācēr-|dōs,
Vīrgĭnĭ-|būs pŭĕ-|rīsquĕ|cāntŏ. *Hor.*

Two other kinds of Compound verse would appear to be used by Boëthius, iv. 5;—the one consisting of an Adonic (8), preceded by a trochaic metre and a syllable; the other also of an Adonic, preceded by an iambic metre and a syllable; the first member of each admitting the usual variations (25, 14); as,

Sīquĭs|Ārctū-|†rī||sīdĕră|nēscīt
Prŏpīn-|quā sūm-||mŏ||cārdĭnĕ|lābī.

Carey followed by Anthon and other eminent *Prosodians*,

speaks of these, as varieties of *Phalæcian Pentameter*,— or according to our classification—of the *Alcmanian Tetrameter Hypercatalectic* (10); but the fact, that Boëthius, throughout the whole of this poem, has regularly used the Trochaïco-Dactylic and the Iambico-Dactylic alternately, with scarcely a departure from the Trochaic law (25) in the one, or from the Iambic law (14) in the other, —forms a weighty objection to this view of the subject.

### RHYMING VERSIFICATION.

☞ The following hymn, written by *Pope Damasus* about the middle of the fourth century, is given as a literary curiosity; not only as affording one of the earliest specimens of rhyming versification so prevalent for many ages afterwards, but also as evidence of the method of reading verse then customary among the Romans. Being written anterior to the decline of the Latin language and while it was yet a living tongue, by one of the most accomplished scholars of his age, it demonstrates beyond contradiction, that *quantity* not *accent* was regarded as the only safe guide in reading or recitation: because, from the structure of the hymn, it is evident, the *Pope* intended his verses to rhyme. Now this they never will do unless read with the nicest attention to quantity in the manner following: viz.—let the first syllable of every line or verse be separated or pointed off, and let the remaining syllables be read and pronounced as Anapæsts; laying a stress on every third syllable; particularly on the final long ones, and we shall have as perfect rhyme as can be desired: thus—

Mār-|tўrĭs éc|cĕ dĭés|Ăgăthǽ,

Vīr-|gĭnĭs é|mĭcăt éx|ĭmĭǽ;
Christus eam sibi quâ sociat,
Et diadema duplex decorat.

Stirpe decens, elegans specie,
Sed magis actibus atque fide,
Terrea prospera nil reputans,
Jussa Dei sibi corde ligans;
Fortior hæc trucibusque viris,
Exposuit sua membra flagris.
Pectore quam fuerit valido,
Torta mamilla docet patulo.
Deliciæ cuï carcer erat;
Pastor ovem Petrus hanc recreat.
Lætior inde, magisque flagrans,
Cuncta flagella cucurrit ovans.
Ethnica turba, rogum fugi*ens*,\*'
Hujus et ipsa meretur o*pem;*\*
Quos fidei titulus decorat,
His Venerem magis ipsa premat.
Jam renitens, quasi sponsa, polo,
Pro misero rogito Damaso.
Sic tua festa coli faciat,
Se celebrantibus ut faveat.

---

\* The possibility if not the probability of making *opem* rhyme with *fugiens* is plausibly argued by Carey. See his *Latin Prosody made Easy, in loc.*

# SUPPLEMENT,

CONTAINING

*Exercises on the Rules of Quantity, Figures of Prosody, and Different Species of Verse,*

FOR GENERAL RECAPITULATION.

| | |
|---|---|
| *Tertĭa* post illas successit *ăēnĕa* proles. | *Ovid.* |
| Omnia jam *fīent, fĭeri* quæ posse negabam. | *Id.* |
| Nam, simul ac species patefacta est verna *diēi.* | *Lucret.* |
| Morbus ut indicat, et *gelidāï* stringor *aquāï.* | *Id.* |
| *Unĭus* ob noxam, et furias Ajacis Oilei. | *Virgil.* |
| Navibus, infandum! amissis, *unĭus* ob iram. | *Id.* |
| Exercet *Dīana* choros, quam mille secutæ. | *Id.* |
| Ira pharetratæ fertur satiata *Dĭanæ.* | *Ovid.* |
| Quam nos\|tro illi\|us la\|batur \| pectore \| vultus. | *Virgil.* |
| Inter cunctantes *cĕcĭdit* moribunda ministros. | *Virgil.* |
| Pyrrhumque, et ingentem *cĕcīdit.* (19.) | *Horace.* |
| Pan deus Arcadiæ *vēnit,* quem *vīdimus* ipsi. | *Virgil.* |
| .. *Vīsa* mihi ante oculos, et *nōtâ* major imago. | *Id.* |
| Hæc ubi dicta *dĕdit* portis sese *extŭlit* ingens. | *Virgil.* |
| .. Demersa exitio.  *Diffīdit* urbium. (32.) | *Horace.* |
| Nam cœlo terras, et terris *abscĭdit*\* undas. | *Ovid.* |
| Matre dea monstrante viam, *dăta* fata secutus. | *Virg.* |
| Cornua *velatārum* obvertimus *antennārum.* | *Id.* |
| Insignem *pietāte vĭrum* tot adire *labōres* . . . | *Id.* |
| . . . . Æolus, et clauso *ventōrum* carc*ĕ*re regnet. | *Id.* |

\* But *abscĭdi,* from *abs* and *cædo,* is long.

## SUPPLEMENT.

Claudite jam rivos *pŭĕri*, sat prata bĭberunt. *Id.*
.... *Alĭtībusque* jaces, nec te in tua *funĕra* mater. *Id.*
Jam nunc *mĭnāci murmŭre* cornuum. ... (24.) *Horace.*
Ipsi in defossis *spĕcŭbus* secura sub altâ. *Virgil.*
Et gener auxilium Priamo *Phrўgĭbusque* ferebat. *Id.*

Et Laberi mimos ut pulchra *poëmătă* mirer. *Horace.*
Et *sălis* occultum referunt in lacte saporem. *Virgil.*
Ecce Dionæi processit *Cæsăris* astrum. *Id.*
Ille, datis *vădĭbus*, ruri qui extractus in urbem est... *Hor.*
Nigranti piceâ, *trăbĭbusque* obscurus acernis. *Virgil.*
Hic Lelegas *Cārasque*, sagittiferosque Gelonos. *Id.*
Flumina jam lactis, jam flumina *nectăris* ibant. *Ovid.*
.... Exspirant acrem *panăces*, absinthia tetra.... *Lucret.*
Armatam *făcĭbus* matrem et serpentibus atris. *Virgil.*

Ut canis in vacuo *lepŏrem* cum Gallicus arvo. *Ovid.*
*Œdĭpŏdas* facito Telegonasque voces. (9.) *Id.*
Munera portantes, *ebŏrisque* aurique talenta. *Virgil.*
Multa super Priamo rogitans, super *Hectŏre* multa. *Id.*
Curculio, atque *inŏpi* metuens formica senectæ. *Id.*
Eoasque acies, et nigri *Memnŏnis* arma. *Id.*
Eripuit, geminique tulit *Chirōnis* in antrum. *Ovid.*
... Aut Helicen jubeo, strictumque *Oriōnis* ensem. *Id.*
Armatumque auro circumspicit *Oriōna*. *Virgil.*
*Immemōres* socii vasti *Cyclōpis* in antro. *Id.*
Mancipiis locuples eget æris *Cappadŏcum* rex. *Horace.*

Ingentem manibus tollit *cratēra* duobus. *Ovid.*
Ingens argentem, Dodonæosque *lebētas*. *Virgil.*
... Junonis, gelidumque *Aniēnem*, et roscida rivis... *Id.*
Non ulli pastos illis egere *diēbus*. *Id.*
Aut impacatos a tergo horrebit *Ibēros*. *Id.*
Jupiter antiqui contraxit tempora *vēris*. *Ovid.*
Æquatæ spirant auræ, datur hora *quiēti*. *Virgil.*
Ascanium surgentem, et spes *hærēdis* Iüli. *Id.*
Nec de *plēbe* deo, sed qui cœlestia magno ... *Ovid.*
... *Rēgis* Romani; primus qui *lēgibus* urbem.... *Virg.*
Fluminibus vertit *vervēcum* lana colorem. *Priscian.*

Tollere consuetas audent *delphīnes* in auras. *Ovid.*
Jam jam contingit summum *radĭce* flagellum. *Catullus.*
Dextera, quæ *Dĭtis* magni sub mœnia tendit. *Virgil.*
Tractavit *calĭcem* manibus dum furta ligurit. *Horace.*
Hinc sinus est longus *Cilĭcum*, qui vergit ad ortus. *Prisc.*
Mœnia conspicio, atque adverso *fornĭce* portas. *Virgil.*
Florentem cytisum, et *salĭces* carpetis amaras. *Id.*
Nec spatio distant *Nesīdum* littora longo. *Priscian.*

*Palūdis* in secreta veniet latibula. (17.) *Phædrus.*
Ambiguam *tellūre* novâ Salamīna futuram. *Horace.*
Una salus victis nullam sperare *salūtem*. *Virgil.*
Nam *Ligŭrum* populos, et magnas rexerat urbes. *Ovid.*
Talis Amyclæi domitus *Pollūcis* habenis. *Virgil.*
Cum faciam vitula pro *frūgibus*, ipse venito. *Id.*

*Trachȳna* video; quis mihi terras dedit. (17.) *Seneca.*
Halcyone *Cëȳca* movet; *Cëȳcis* in ore . . . . *Ovid.*
Sive *Erȳcis* fines regemque optatis Acesten. *Virgil.*

. . . *Conserĭmus*, multos Danaum *demittĭmus* Orco. *Id.*
*Fudĭmus*, insidiis, totâque *agitavĭmus* urbe. *Id.*
Cæca *sequēbātur*, totumque incauta per agmen . . . . *Id.*
Lac *facitōte* bibat, nostrâque sub arbore ludat. *Ovid.*
. . . *Scriptūrus;* neque te ut *mirētur* turba labores. *Hor.*
*Solūtus* omni fœnore. (20.) *Id.*

Hoc erat, hoc votis inquit quod sæpe *petīvi*. *Virgil.*
Sed quamvis formæ nunquam mihi fama *petīta* est. *Ovid.*
Nec tamen, et cuncti miserum servare *velītis*. *Id.*
Nec miseræ prodesse in tali tempore *quībat*. *Lucretius.*
*Viderītis* stellas illic ubi circulus axem . . . . *Ovid.*
Dein cum millia multa *fecerīmus*. (29.) *Catullus.*

. . . Limina portarum, nec spes opis ulla *dăbātur*. *Virg.*

Troja per undosum *petĕrētur* classibus æquor. *Virgil.*
Sanguine fœdantum quos ipse *sacravĕrat* ignes. *Id.*
Carmina tum melius, cum *venĕrit* ipse canemus. *Id.*
Si modo fert animus, *gradĕre*, et *scitabĕre* ab ipso. *Ovid.*

"Noris nos" inquit; docti sŭmus." Hic ego, "Pluris."
*Horace.*

*Dexterā* diriguit, nec *citrā, motă* nec ultra. *Ovid.*
Sed tamen iste deus qui sit *dā* Tityre nobis. *Virgil.*

... Leniit, et *tacitā* refluens *ită* substitit, undâ ... *Vir.*

*Solvitĕ cordĕ* metum Teucri, *secluditĕ* curas. *Virgil.*
*Molў* vocant superi; nigrâ *radicĕ* tenetur. *Ovid.*

*Nesæē* Spioque, Thaliaque, *Cymodocēque.* *Virgil.*
Pro *rē* pauca loquar. Nec ego hanc abscondere furto ... *Id.*
Vos *Tempē* totidem tollite laudibus (32.) *Horace.*
Consiliis *parē*, quæ nunc pulcherrima Nantes. ... *Virgil.*
*Mē* miserum! *nē* prona cadas, *indignavĕ* lædi. *Ovid.*
*Certē* sive mihi *P*hyllis, sive esset Amyntas ... *Virgil.*
Non *benĕ* cœlestes impia dextra colit. (9.) *Ovid.*
Tecta *supernĕ* timent, metuunt *infernĕ* cavernas. ...
*Lucretius.*

*Vidī* Virgineas intumuisse genas. (9.) *Ovid.*
*Vultū* quo cœlum tempestatesque serenat. *Virgil.*

O crudelis *Alexī*, nihil mea carmina curas. *Virgil.*
*Sicutī* summarum summa est æterna, neque extra....
*Lucretius.*
Est *mihī*, sitque precor, flavæ tutela Minervæ. ... *Ovid.*
*P*uella senibus dulcior *mihī*\* cygnis. (23.) *Martial.*
Nec jacere *indŭ* manus, via qua munita fidēi. *Lucretius.*

Victa jacet pietas, et *Virgō* cæde madentes. ... *Ovid.*
Cadet in terras *Virgō* relictas. (12.) *Seneca.*
*Orō*, qui reges consuesti tollere, cur non. ... *Horace.*
Quo fugis? *Orŏ*† mane, nec me, crudelis, amantem. ...
*Ovid.*

---

\* Decisive instances of *mihi, tibi,* &c., with the final *i* long, occur frequently in Iambic verse. See Plaut. Cist. II. 3. 11. Pœnul. I. 3. 3. Catul. 42. 8. (al, 45. 8.); 23. 6. (al. 25. 6.); 8. 3. 15. Hor. Epod. 4. 2; 5. 101; 8. 3; 10. 16; 15, 20. Phæd. III. prol. 61; 12. 7. II. 4. 7. III. 18. 14. IV. 6, 24. II. 5. 4. III. 18. 2. Hor. Carm. IV. 5. 6, &c.

† See Ov. Met. II. 566. III. 266. XV. 497. Trist. I. 1. 44; 2. 77. Am. III. 7. 2. Hor. Sat. I. 4. 104, &c.

## SUPPLEMENT. 117

Sed timuit, ne forte sacer *tŏt ăb* ignibus æther... *Ovid.*
Hic *vĕl ăd* Elei metas et maxima campi... *Virgil.*
Tum *patĕr* omnipotens misso *perfregĭt* Olympum... *Ov.*

*Vēr* erat æternum, placidique tepentibus auris.. *Id.*
... Si cita dissiliant nempe *āēr* omne necesse est....
*Lucretius.*
Dum calet, et medio *sōl* est altissimus orbe. *Ovid.*
Sisyphon aspiciens, "*cūr* hic e fratribus" inquit... *Id.*

*Sīc* omnes, ut et ipsa Jovis conjuxque sororque... *Ov.*
... Ulla tenent, unco *nōn* alligat anchora morsu. *Virgil.*

Quid vetat irato *numĕn* adesse deo? (9.) *Ovid.*
*Daphnĭn* ad astra feremus; amavit nos quoque Daphnis.
*Virgil.*
*Iliŏn* in Tyriam transfer felicius urbem. *Ovid.*
*Donĕc* eris felix multos numerabis amicos. *Id.*
*Forsităn* et nostrum nomen miscebitur istis. *Id.*

Aut tondit *infirmās* oves. (20.) *Horace.*
*Matrēs* atque viri, defunctaque corpora vitâ. *Virgil.*
Virginibus Tyriis *mōs* est gestare pharetram. *Id.*
Siquĭs erit qui te, quod sis *meŭs* esse legendum... *Ovid.*
... Et *Libȳs* Amphimedon, avidi committere pugnam. *Id.*

Vivitur ex rapto; non *hospĕs* ab hospĭte tutus. *Ovid.*
Ultus *ĕs* offensas, ut decet, ipse tuas. (9.) *Id.*

Queruntur in *sylvīs* aves. (20.) *Horace.*
... *Currūs* et intactas boves. (20.) *Id.*
*Vīs* ut nulla virûm, non ipsi excindere ferro... *Virgil.*
... Cum *sīs* et prave sectum stomacheris ob unguem.
*Horace.*
Ter vocata *audīs*, adimisque letho. (28.) *Id.*
*Quamvīs* increpitent socii, et vi cursus in altum... *Virg.*
Hic situs est *P*haëthon, *c*urrūs auriga paterni. *Ovid.*
Fiet enim subito *sūs* horridus atraque tigris. *Virgil.*
Nare per æstatem liquidam *suspexerĭs* agmen. *Id.*

Si thure *placarīs* et hornâ ... (19.)  *Horace.*
... Sors exitura, et nos in *æternum*\* (19.)
Exilium impositura cymbæ. (42.)  *Horace.*

1. Terras|que trac|tusque maris cœlumque profundum.
2. Amphi|on Dir|cæus in | Actæ|ō Ara|cyntho.
3. Nec *sum* adeo informis nuper me in littore vidi.
4. Te Corydon ŏ A|lexī : trahit sua quemque voluptas.
5. Et longum formose vălē vălē inquit Iola.
6. Tityre pascentes a flumine | reice ca|pellas.
7. Clara Deum Soboles, magnum Jovis | incre|mentum.
8. Cum gravius dorso subi|īt onus. | Incipit ille.
9. Pro molli viola pro purpure|o nar|cisso.
10. Flŭviorum rex Eridanus, camposque per omnes.
11. Ter sunt cona|ti im|ponere | Pelio Ossam.
12. Glauco, | et Pano|peæ et | Ino|o Meli|certæ.
13. Insulæ | Ioni|o in mag|no, quas dira Celæno.
14. Et spu|mas miscent ar|genti, | vivaque | sulphur*a*—
   Idæasque pices.
15. Sed fortuna valens audacem fecerat | Orph*ea*.
16. Bis patriæ cecidere manus. Quin protinus | omn*ia*.
17. Stant et | junipe|ri & | castane|æ hir|sutæ.

1. Que long by Cæsura, see p. 73.
2. In the fifth foot *o* is not elided. See under Synalæpha, p. 76.
3. In this verse three elisions.
4. O is not elided. See under Synalæpha.
5. The *e* in the 2d *vale* not elided but shortened. See under Synalæpha.
6. Either to be read *rej'ce* by Syncope of *i;* or the *j* elided, and then *reïce* contracted into *reice* by Synæresis, p. 74.
7. This is a Spondaic Hexameter.
8. *it onus*—*it* long by Cæsura.
9. A Spondaic Hexameter.
10. *Fluviorum* to be read as if *fluvjorum*, or taken as an Anapæst.
11. In two vowels of this line Synalæpha not employed.
12. Do. and a diphthong shortened.
13. In the first foot a diphthong not elided but shortened.
14. *A* at the end is elided by the vowel at the commencement of the next line.
15. Pronounce the last word *Orpha* by Crasis, p. 75.
16. *Omnia* made two syllables.
17. This line a Spondaic, and has two vowels unelided by Synalæphe.

\* To be read "*æter-*||*N exilium.*"

# APPENDIX,

CONTAINING

# STIRLING'S RHETORIC;

IN

# LATIN AND ENGLISH.

# ARS RHETORICA.

Tropi proprii Quatuor.

Dat propriæ similem, translata *Metaphora* vocem,    1
Atque *Metonymia* imponit nova nomina rebus.    2
Confundit totum cum parte *Synecdoche* sæpe.    3

### EXEMPLA.

1. Fluctuat *æstu* (i. e. excessu), irarum. *Aspirant* (i. e. favent) cœptis. 2. Inventor *pro* Invento; ut *Mars* (i. e. bellum) sævit. Author *pro* Operibus; ut, lego H*oratium*, (i. e. ejus scripta.) Instrumentum *pro* Causâ; ut, *lingua* (i. e. eloquentia) tuetur illum. Materia *pro* Facto; ut, *ferrum*, (i. e. gladius) vicit. Effectus *pro* Causâ; ut, *frigida* mors, (i. e. quæ facit frigidos.) Continens *pro* Contento; ut, vescor *dapibus*, (i, e. cibis.) Adjunctum *pro* Subjecto; ut, *fasces*, (i. e. magistratus). 3. Decem *æstates*, (i. e. annos) vixi sub hoc tecto, (i. e. domo.) Nunc *annus*, (i. e. ver) est formosissimus.

### DERIVATIONES.

1. à μεταφέρω, transfero. 2. à μετονομάζω, transnomino. 3. à συνεκδέχομαι, comprehendo.

# THE
# ART OF RHETORIC.

### The four proper Tropes.

| | |
|---|---|
| A *Metaphor*, in place of proper words, | 1 |
| Resemblance puts; and dress to speech affords. | |
| A *Metonymy* does new names impose, | 2 |
| And Things for things by near relation shows. | |
| *Synecdoche* the Whole for *P*art does take, | 3 |
| Or *P*art for Whole; just for the metre's sake. | |

### EXAMPLES.

1. He boils with a *Tide* (i. e. Excess) of *P*assion. They *breathe on* (i. e. favour) my Enterprises. 2. The Inventor is taken for the Invented; as, *Mars* (i. e. War) rages. The Author for his Works; as, I read H*o*race, (i. e. his Writings.) The Instrument for the Cause; as, his *Tongue* (i. e. Eloquence) defends him. The matter for the Thing made; as, the *Steel* (i. e. Sword) conquers. The effect for the Cause; as, c*o*ld Death, (i. e. Death that makes cold.) The subject containing for the Thing contained; I feed on *dainties*, (i. e. on food.) The adjunct for the subject; as, *the Mace* (i. e. Magistrate) comes. 3. Ten *Summers* (i. e. Years) I have lived under this Roof, (i. e. House.) Now the *Year* (i. e. Spring) is the most beautiful.

### TERMS ENGLISHED.

1. Translation. 2. Changing of Names. 3. Comprehension.

Contrà quàm sentit solet *Ironia* jocari. 4

## Affectiones Troporum.

Durior impropriæ est *Catachresis* abusio vocis. 5
Extenuans, augensve, excedit *Hyperbole* verum. 6
Voce Tropos plures nectit *Metalepsis* in unâ. 7
Continuare Tropos *Allegoria* adsolet usque. 8

## Tropi falsò habiti.

*Antonomasia* imponit Cognomina sæpe. 9

### EXEMPLA.

4. *Benè* factum, (i. e. malè factum.)  5. *Vir* gregis, (i. e. dux gregis.) *Minatur*, (i. e. promittit) pulchra. 6. Currit *ocior Euro*, (i. e. citissime.)  7. *Euphrates*, (i. e. Mesopotamia, i. e. ejus incolæ), movet bellum. 8. *Venus*, (i. e. amor) friget sine *Cerere*, (i. e. pane) & *Baccho*, (i. e. vino.)  9. Hic adest *Irus*, (i. e. pauper.) *Æacides*, (i. e. Achilles) vicit. *Pœnus*, (i. e. Hannibal) tulit victoriam. *Cytherea*, (i. e. Venus, Dea insulæ Cytheræ.) *Philosophus*, (i. e. Aristoteles) asserit. *Poeta*, (i. e. Virgilius) canit Æneam.

### DERIVATIONES.

4. ab εἰρωνεύομαι, dissimulo.  5. à καταχράομαι, abutor.  6. ab ὑπερβάλλω, supero.  7. à μεταλαμβάνω, participo.  8. ab ἀλληγορέω, aliud dico.  9. ab ἀντί, pro, & ὀνομάζω, nomino.

And *Irony*, dissembling with an air, 4
Thinks otherwise than what the words declare.

### Affections of Tropes.

A *Catachresis* words too far doth strain: 5
Rather from such abuse of speech refrain.
*Hyperbole* soars too high or creeps too low: 6
Exceeds the truth, things wonderful to show.
By *Metalepsis*, in one word combin'd, 7
More Tropes than one you easily may find.
An *Allegory* tropes continues still, 8
Which with new graces every sentence fill.

### Tropes improperly accounted so.

*Antonomasia* proper names imparts 9
From kindred, country, epithets, or arts.

#### EXAMPLES.

4. *Fairly* done, (i. e. scandalously done.) Good Boy, (i. e. Bad Boy.) 5. The *Man*, (i. e. Chief) of the Flock. He *threatens*, (i. e. promises) a favour. 6. He runs *swifter than the wind*, (i. e. very swiftly.) 7. *Euphrates*, (i. e. Mesopotamia, i. e. its Inhabitants) moves War. 8. *Venus* grows cold without *Ceres* and *Bacchus*, i. e. (Love grows cold without Bread and Wine.) 9. There goes *Irus*, (i. e. a poor Man.) *Æacides* (i. e. Achilles) conquered. The *Carthaginian*, (i. e. Hannibal) won the Field. *Cytherea*, (i. e. Venus worshipped in the Island so called.) The *Philosopher*, (i. e. Aristotle) asserted so. The *Poet*, (i. e. Virgil) sings of Æneas.

#### TERMS ENGLISHED.

4. Dissimulation. 5. Abuse. 6. Excess. 7. Participation. 8. Speaking otherwise. 9. For a name.

Si plus quàm dicis signes, *Litotes* vocabis. 10
A sonitu voces *Onomatopœia* fingit. 11
*Antiphrasis* voces tibi per contraria signat. 12
Dat *Charientismus* pro duris mollia verba. 13
*Asteismus* jocus urbanus, seu scomma facetum est. 14
Est inimica viri *Diasyrmus* abusio vivi. 15
Insultans·hosti illudit *Sarcasmus* amarè. 16
Si quid proverbî fertur *Parœmia* dicta est. 17

### EXEMPLA.

10. *Non laudo tua munera nec sperno*, (i. e. vitupero ea tamen accipio). 11. *Tinnitus* æris; *rugitus* leonum. 12. *Lucus*, à luceo, significat opacum nemus. 13. Ad bona verba precor: ne sævi, magna Sacerdos. 14. Qui Bavium non odit, amet tua carmina Mævi: atque idem jungat vulpes, & mulgeat hircos. 15. In strepitu cantas: digna sed argutos interstrepere anser olores. 16. Satia te sanguine, Cyre. 17. *Lupum auribus teneo.*

### DERIVATIONES.

10. à λιτὸς, tenuis. 11. ab ὀνοματοποιέω, nomen facio. 12. ab ἀντιφράζω, per contrarium loquor. 13. à χαριεντίζομαι, jocor. 14. ab ἀςεῖος, urbanus. 15. à διασύρω, convitior. 16. á σαρκάζω, irrideo. 17. à παροιμιάζομαι, proverbialiter loquor.

*Litotes* doth more sense than words include,    10
And often by two negatives hath stood.
*Onomatopœia* coins words from sound,    11
By which alone the meaning may be found.
*Antiphrasis* makes words to disagree    12
From sense; if rightly they derived be.
*Charientismus*, when it speaks, doth choose    13
The softer for the harsher words to use.
*Asteismus* loves to jest with strokes of wit,    14
And slily with the point of satire hit.
A *Diasyrmus* must ill nature show,    15
And ne'er omits t' insult a living foe.
*Sarcasmus* with a biting jeer doth kill,    16
And every word with strongest venom fill.
*Parœmia* by a *P*roverb tries to teach    17
A short, instructing, and a nervous speech.

### EXAMPLES.

10. *I neither praise your Gifts, nor despise them*, (i. e. I dispraise your Gifts, yet I accept them.) 11. *The tinkling* of brass; *the roaring* of lions. 12. *Lucus*, from *Lux*, Light, signifies a dark shady Grove. 13. Be not so angry: Heaven send better News. 14. Who hates not Bavius, let him love Mævius' verses; and he that loves either, let him yoke foxes and milk the He-goats. 15. You cackle like a Goose among the tuneful Swans. 16. Now Cyrus, glut yourself with Blood. 17. I know not what to do.

### TERMS ENGLISHED.

10. Lessening. 11. Feigning a name. 12. Contrary Word. 13. Softening. 14. Civility. 15. Detraction. 16. Bitter Taunt. 17. A Proverb.

*Ænigma* obscuris tecta est sententia verbis.     18

### Figuræ Dictionis in eodem Sono.

Dat varium sensum voci *Antanaclasis* eidem.     19
Atque *Ploce* repetit proprium; communiter hocce.     20
Diversis membris frontem dat *Anaphora* eandem.     21
Complures clausus concludit *Epistrophe* eodem.     22
*Symploce* eas jungit, complexa utramque figuram.     23
Incipit et voce exit *Epanalepsis* eâdem.     24
Est *Anadiplosis* cùm quæ postrema prioris     25
Vox est, hæc membri fit dictio prima sequentis.

#### EXEMPLA

18. *Arundo Nilotis*, (i. e. Papyrus Nili) profert *filiolas Cadmi*, (i. e. Græcas literas inventas ab illo.) 19. Quis neget Æneæ natum de stirpe Neronem? *Sustulit* hic matrem, *sustulit* ille patrem! 20. In hâc victoriâ Cæsar erat *Cæsar*, (i. e. mitissimus victor.) 21. *Pax* coronat vitam : *pax* profert copiam. 22. Nascimur *dolore*, degimus vitam *dolore*, finimus *dolore*. 23. *Quis* legem tulit? *Rullus*. *Quis* majorem populi partem suffragiis privavit? *Rullus*. *Quis* comitiis præfuit? Idem *Rullus*. 24. *Multa* super Priamo rogitans, super Hectore *multa*. 25. Hic tamen *vivit* : *Vivit?* imo vero etiam in senatum venit.

#### DERIVATIONES.

18 ab αἰνίττω, obscurè loquor. 19. ab ἀντανακλάω, refringo. 20. à πλέκω, necto. 21. ab ἀναφέρω, refero. 22. ab ἐπιςρέφω, converto. 23. à συμπλέκω, connecto. 24. ab ἐπὶ, & ἀναλαμβάνω, repeto. 25. ab ἀναδιπλόω, reduplico.

## ART OF RHETORIC. 127

*Ænigma* in dark words the sense conceals;     18
But, that once known, a riddling speech reveals.
           FIGURES of Words of the same sound.
*Antanaclasis* in one sound contains     19
More meanings, which the various sense explains.
By *Ploce* one a proper name repeats;     20
Yet as a common noun the latter treats.
*Anaphora* gives more sentences one head;     21
As readily appear to those that read.
*Epistrophe* more sentences doth close     22
With the same words, whether in verse or prose.
*Symploce* joins these figures both together,     23
And from both join'd makes up itself another.
*Epanalepsis* words doth recommend,     24
The same at the beginning and the end.
*Anadiplosis* ends the former line     25
With what the next does for its first design.

              EXAMPLES.

18. *Nilotis's Quill* brought forth the Daughters of Cadmus, (i. e. a Pen made of a Reed growing by the side of the River Nile wrote the Greek Letters invented by Cadmus.) 19. Who can deny that Nero is descended from Æneas? The former *took off* (i. e. killed) his mother; the latter *took off* (i. e. affectionately removed from danger) his father. 20. In that Victory Cæsar was *Cæsar*, (i. e. a most serene Conqueror.) 21. *P*eace crowns our Life; *P*eace does our *P*lenty breed. 22. We are born in *Sorrow;* pass our time in *Sorrow;* end our days in *Sorrow.* 23. *Who* proposed the law? *Rullus.* *Who* deprived the majority of the people of their right of suffrage? *Rullus.* *Who* presided at the comitia? The same identical *Rullus.* 24. *Many* questions anxiously asking about *P*riam, about Hector, *many.* 25. And yet this man is permitted *to live:—to live?* Yea, and even to come into the senate!

             TERMS ENGLISHED.

18. A Riddle. 19. A Reciprocation. 20. Continuation. 21. Rehearsal. 22. A turning to. 23. A Complication. 24. Repetition. 25. Reduplication.

Prima velut mediis, mediis ita *Epanados* ima 26
Consona dat repetens.  Exemplo disce figuram.
Ejusdem fit *Epizeuxis* repetitio vocis. 27
Continuâ serie est repetita gradatio *Climax*. 28
Estque *Polyptoton* vario si dictio casu. 29

### Figuræ Dictionis similis Soni.

Fonte ab eodem derivata *Paragmenon* aptat. 30
Voce parùm mutatâ, alludit significatum.
*Paranomasia:* ut " amentis non gestus amantis." 31
Fine sono similes conjungit H*omoioteleuton*. 32
Inque *Parechesi* repetita est Syllaba vocum. 33

#### EXEMPLA.

26. *Crudelis* tu quoque *mater; crudelis mater* magis, an *puer improbus ille? Improbus ille puer, crudelis* tu quoque *mater*. 27. Ah! *Corydon, Corydon.*\* *Bella,* horrida *bella*. 28. Quod *libet*, id *licet*, his; at quod *licet*, id satis *audent*; quodque *audent, faciunt; faciunt* quodcunque molestum est. 29. Arma armis; pedi pes; viro vir. 30. Pieridum studio *studiosè* teneris. 31. *Amentis* non gestus *amantis;* ut supra. 32. Si vis incolumen, si vis te reddere *sanum*, curas tolle graves, irasci crede *profanum*. 33. *O fortunatam natam.*

#### DERIVATIONES.

26. ab ἐπὶ, & ἄνοδος, ascensus. 27. ab ἐπιζεύγνυμι, conjungo. 28. à κλίνω, acclino. 29. à πολὺς, varius, & πτῶσις, casus. 30. à παράγω, derivo. 31. à παρὰ, juxta, & ὄνομα. nomen. 32. ab ὁμοίως, similiter, & τέλευτον, finitum. 33. à παρηχέω, sono similis sum.

---

\* In translating some of these figures, it is extremely difficult—owing to idiomatic phraseology, dissimilarity of sound, &c., &c.,—to give more than equivalent sense; as in the present example, and many others farther on.

By *Epanados* a sentence shifts its place,     26
Takes first, and last, and also middle space.
An *Epizeuxis* twice a word repeats,     27
Whate'er the theme or subject be it treats.
A *Climax* by gradation still ascends,     28
Until the sense with finished period ends.
A *Polyptoton* still the same word places,     29
If sense requires it, in two different cases.

FIGURES of Words of like Sound.

*Paragmenon* derived from one recites     30
More words; and in one sentence them unites.
*Paronomasia* to the sense alludes,     31
When words but little vary'd it includes.
*Homoioteleuton* makes the measure chime     32
With like sounds in the end of fetter'd rhyme.
A *Parachesis* syllable sets twice;     33
But this, except to poets, is a vice.

### EXAMPLES.

26. Whether *the worst?* the *Child accurst*, or else the *cruel mother?* The *Mother worst*, the *Child accurst;* as bad the one as t'other. 27. Ah! *poor, poor* Swain! *Wars*, horrid *wars.* 28. *Folly* breeds *Laughter; Laughter, Disdain; Disdain* makes *Shame her Daughter.* 29. Foot to foot; Hand to Hand; Face to Face. 30. I write *friendly* of Friendship to a Friend. 31. *Friends* are turned *fiends.* 32. Chime and Rhyme, as above. 33. Liberty begets *Mischief chiefly.*

### TERMS ENGLISHED.

26. A Regression. 27. A joining together. 28. A Ladder, Stair. 29. Variation of Case. 30. Derived from the same. 31. Likeness of Words. 32. A like ending. 33. Allusion.

## Figuræ ad Explicationem.

| | |
|---|---|
| Exprimit atque oculis quasi subjicit *Hypotyposis*. | 34 |
| Res, loca, personas, affectus, tempora, gestus. | |
| Explicat oppositum addens *Paradiastole* rectè. | 35 |
| Opposita *Antimetabole* mutat dictaque sæpe. | 36 |
| Librat in Antithetis contraria *Enantiosis*. | 37 |
| *Synœceiosis* duo dat contraria eidem. | 38 |
| *Oxymoron* " iners erit ars ;" " Concordia discors." | 39 |

## Figuræ ad Probationem.

| | |
|---|---|
| *Propositi* reddit causas *Ætiologia*. | 40 |
| Arguit allatam rem contra *Inversio* pro se. | 41 |

### EXEMPLA.

34. Videbar videre alios intrantes, alios verò exeuntes; quosdam ex vino vacillantes, quasdam hesternâ potatione oscitantes, &c. 35. Fortuna obumbrat virtutem, tamen non obruit eam. 36. Poëma est *pictura loquens*, pictura est *mutum poëma.* 37. *Alba* ligustra cadunt, vaccinia *nigra* leguntur. 38. Tam *quod adest* desit quam *quod non adsit* avaro. 39. Superba humilitas. 40. Sperne voluptates: *nocet empta dolore voluptas.* 41. Imò equidem: neque enim, si occidissem, sepelissem.

### DERIVATIONES.

34. ab ὑποτυπόω, repræsento. 35. à παραδιαϛέλλω, disjungo. 36. ab ἀντὶ, contrà, & μεταβάλλω, inverto. 37. ab ἐναντίος, oppositus. 38. à συνοικειῶ, concilio. 39. ab ὀξὺ, acutum, & μωρὸν, stultum. 40. ab αἰτιολογέω, rationem reddo. 41. ab *inverto*.

### Figures for Explanation.

*Hypotyposis* to the eye contracts    34
Things, places, persons, affections, acts.
*Paradiastole* explains aright    35
Things in an opposite and diff'rent light.
*Antimetabole* puts chang'd words again    36
By contraries; as the example will explain.
*Enantiosis* poiseth diff'rent things,    37
And words and sense as into balance brings.
*Synœceiosis* to one subject ties    38
Two contraries; and fuller sense supplies.
In *Oxymoron* contradictions meet:    39
And jarring epithets and subjects greet.

### Figures for Proof.

*Ætiology* gives every theme a reason;    40
For sure that never can be out of season.
*Inversion* makes the adversary's plea    41
A strong nay best defence that urg'd can be.

#### EXAMPLES.

34. The Head is sick; the Heart is faint; from the sole of the Foot, even, unto the Head, there is no soundness, but Wounds, Bruises, and putrefying sores. 35. Virtue may be overshadowed, but not overwhelmed. 36. A poem is a *speaking Picture;* a Picture is a *mute Poem.* 37. *Truth* brings *Foes, Flattery* brings *Friends.* 38. He is dead even *while he liveth..* 39. Proud humility. This bitter sweet. 40. Despise Pleasures, for *Pleasure bought with pain hurteth.* 41. Had I killed him, (as you report,) I had not staid to bury him.

#### TERMS ENGLISHED.

34. A Representation. 35. Discrimination. 36. Changing by Contraries. 37. A Contrariety. 38. Reconciling. 39. A witty foolish saying. 40. Showing a Reason. 41. Inversion.

Anticipat, quæ quis valet objecisse, *Prolepsis.* 42
Planè aut dissimulans permittit *Epitrope* factum. 43

## Figuræ ad Amplificationem.

Ad summum ex imo gradibus venit *Incrementum.* 44
Verba *Synonymia* addit rem signantia eandem. 45
Res specie varias *Synathræsmus* congerit unà. 46
" Non dico," *Apophasis ;* " Taceo, mitto," est *Paraleipsis.* 47

### EXEMPLA.

42. Hic aliquis mihi dicat: cur ego amicum offendam in nugis? hæ nugæ seria ducunt in mala. 43. Credo equidem: neque te teneo, nec dicta refello. 44. Justum et tenacem propositi virum non civium ardor prava jubentium, non vultus instantis Tyranni, mente quatit solida, neque Auster dux inquieti turbidus Adriæ, nec fulminantis magna manus Jovis; si fractus illabatur orbis, impavidum ferient ruinæ. 45. Ensis & gladius. Vivit & vescitur æthereâ aurâ. 46. Grammaticus, Rhetor, *P*ictor, Aliptes, Augur, Schœnobates, Medicus, Magus: omnia novit. 47. *Non referam* ignaviam & alia magis scelesta, quorum pœnitere oportet. 47. *Taceo ; mitto* homicidia, furta, & alia tua crimina.

### DERIVATIONES

42. à προλαμβάνω, anticipo. 43. ab ἐπιτρέπω, permitto. 44. ab *incresco*. 45. á σὺν, con, & ὄνομα, nomen. 46. à συναθροίζω, congrego. 47. ab ἀπὸ, ab, & φάω, dico ;— a παραλείπω, prætermitto.

*Prolepsis* your objection doth prevent,     42
With answers suitable and pertinent.
*Epitrope* gives leave, and facts permits,     43
Whether it speaks sincere, or counterfeits.

### Figures for Amplifying.

An *Incrementum* by degrees doth rise,     44
And from a low t' a lofty pitch it flies.
*Synonymy* doth divers words prepare,     45
Yet each of them one meaning doth declare.
A *Synathræsmus* sums up various things,     46
And as into one heap together brings.
*Apophasis*, pretending to conceal     47
The whole it meant to hide, must needs reveal.
A *Paraleipsis* cries; "I leave't behind,     47
I let it pass;" tho' you the whole may find.

### EXAMPLES.

42. What then? shall we sin, because we are not under the Law, but Grace? God forbid. 43. Go, take your Course, I will not stop your Rambles. 44. The Wickedness of a Mob, the cruel Force of a Tyrant, Storms and Tempests, even Jupiter's Thunder; nay, if the World should fall, it cannot disturb the just Man, nor shake his solid Resolution. 45. Freedom and Li ert ; He is yet alive; he breathes æthereal Air. 46. Thief, Tailor, Miller, Weaver, &c. 47. *I say nothing* of your Idleness, and other Things, for which you cannot excuse yourself. 47. *I omit* the Bribes you received; *I let pass* your Thefts, your Robberies, and your other crimes.

### TERMS ENGLISHED.

42. Prevention. 43. Permission. 44. Increasing. 45. Partaking together of a Name. 46. Gathering together. 47. Not saying. 47. Leaving.

Rem circumloquitur per plura *Periphrasis* unam. 48
*Hendiadys* fixum dat mobile, sic duo fixa. 49

### Ad Affectuum Concitationem.

Quærit *Erotesis*, poterat quod dicere rectè. 50
Concitat *Ecphonesis* & *Exclamatio* mentem. 51
Narratæ subit & rei *Epiphonema* probatæ. 52
Est *Epanorthosis* positi correctio sensus. 53
*Aposiopesis* sensa imperfecta relinquit. 54
Consultat cum aliis *Anacœnosis* ubique. 55
Consulit addubitans quid agat dicatve *Aporia*. 56

### EXEMPLA.

48. *Scriptor Trojani belli*, (i. e. Homerus.) 49. Bibit ex auro & pateris, *pro* aureis pateris. 50. Creditis avectos hostes? aut ulla putatis dona carere dolis Danaûm? 51. Heu *P*ietas! heu prisca fides! heu vana voluptas! 52. Tantæ molis erat Romanam condere gentem. 53. O clementia! clementia dixi? potius patientia mira. 54. Quos ego——sed motos præstat componere fluctus. 55. Si ita haberet se tua res quid concilii aut rationis inires? 56. Quid faciam? roger, anne rogem? quid deinde rogabo?

### DERIVATIONES.

48. à περιφράζω, circumloquor. 49 ab ἕν, unum, διὰ, per, & δυο, duo. 50. ab ἐρωτάω, interrogo. 51. ab ἐκφωνέω, exclamo. 52. ab ἐπιφωνέω, acclamo. 53. ab ἐπανορθόω, corrigo. 54. ab ἀπὸ, post, & σιωπάω, obticeo. 55. ab ἀνακοινόω, communico. 56. ab ἀπορέω, addubito.

*Periphrasis* of words doth use a train, 48
Intending one thing only to explain.
H*endiadys* turns to substantives, you'll see, 49
What adjectives with substantives agree.

### TO ROUSE THE FEELINGS.

By *Erotesis* what we know we ask, 50
Prescribing to ourselves a needless task.
By *Ecphonesis* straight the mind is raised, 51
When by a sudden flow of passion seiz'd.
*Epiphonema* makes a final clause, 52
When narratives and proofs afford a cause.
*Epanorthosis* doth past words correct, 53
And only to enhance seems to reject.
*Aposiopesis* leaves imperfect sense; 54
Yet such a silent pause speaks eloquence.
*Anacœnosis* tries another's mind, 55
The better counsel of a friend to find.
*Aporia* in words and actions doubts, 56
And with itself what may be best disputes.

### EXAMPLES.

48. *The writer of the Trojan War* (*for* Homer). 49. He drinks out of Gold and Cups, *for* Golden Cups. 50. Do you imagine the enemy departed? Do you believe any boons from the Greeks free from wile? 51. Alas! Oh banished *P*iety! Oh corrupted Nation! 52. Of so great Moment was it to raise the Roman Nation. 53. Most brave! Brave, said I? Most heroic Act. 54. Whom I— but it is better to compose the swelling waves. 55. Were it your case, what would you do? 56. What shall I do; must I be asked, or must I ask? Then what shall I ask?

### TERMS ENGLISHED.

48. Circumlocution. 49. One in two. 50. A Questioning—Interrogation. 51. Exclamation. 52. Acclamation. 53. Correcting. 54. A Pausing or Concealing. 55. A Communication. 56. A Doubting.

Personam inducit *Prosopopœia* loquentem.  57
Sermonem à præsenti avertit *Apostrophe* ritè.  58

## Schemata Grammatica ORTHOGRAPHIÆ.

*Prosthesis* apponit capiti; sed *Aphæresis* aufert.  59
*Syncope* de medio tollit; sed *Epenthesis* addit.  60
Abstrahit *Apocope* fini; sed dat *Paragoge*.  61

### EXEMPLA.

57. Hosne mihi fructus, hunc fertilitas honorem officiique refers? (Tellus fingitur loqui.) 58. Et auro vi potitur. Quid non mortalia pectora cogis, auri sacra fames? 59. Gnatus, *pro* natus; non temnere, *pro* non contemnere Divos. 60. Surrêxe, *pro* surrexisse;—Mavors, *pro* Mars. 61. Ingeni, *pro* ingenii;—vestirier, *pro* vestiri.

### DERIVATIONES.

57. à πρόσωπον, persona, & ποιέω, facio. 58. ab ἀποςρέφω, verto. 59. à προςίθημι, appono;—ab ἀφαιρέω, aufero. 60. à σὺν, con, & κόπτω, scindo;—ab ἐπὶ, in, & ἐντίθημι, infero. 61. ab ἀπὸ, ab, & κόπτω, scindo;—à παρὰ, præter, & ἄγω, duco.

*Prosopopeia* a new person feigns,    57
And to inanimates speech and reason deigns.
*Apostrophe* for greater themes or less    58
Doth turn aside, to make a short address.

### Figures of Orthography.

*Prosthesis* to the front of words doth add    59
Letters or syllables they never had.
*Aphæresis* from the beginning takes    59
What syllable or letter the word up-makes.
*Syncope* leaves the middle syllable out,    60
Which causes oft of case and tense to doubt.
*Epenthesis* to middle adds one more    60
Than what the word could justly claim before.
*Apocope* cuts off a final letter,    61
Or syllable, to make the verse run better.
A *Paragoge* adds unto the end,    61
Yet not the sense, but measure to amend.

### EXAMPLES.

57. The very Stones of the Street speak your Wickedness. The Mountains clap their Hands, and the Hills sing for Joy. 58. Thus he possessed the gold by Violence. Oh! cursed Thirst of Gold, what wickedness dost thou not influence men's minds to perpetrate? 59. 'Yclad in Armour, *for* clad; begirt *for* girt with a Sword. 59. Till *for* until. 60. Ne'er *for* never; o'er *for* over;—Blackamoor *for* Blackmoor. 61. Tho' *for* though;—Chicken *for* Chick.

### TERMS ENGLISHED.

57. Feigning a *P*erson—Personification. 58. An Address, or turning away from the principal Subject. 59. Adding to. 59. Taking from. 60. Cutting out;—Interposition. 61. A cutting off;—Producing, or making longer.

*Metathesis* sedem commutat Literularum. 62
Literulam *Antithesis* ipsam mutare paratur. 63

### Syntaxeos in Excessu.

Vocibus exsuperat *Pleonasmus* & emphasin auget. 64
Conjunctura frequens vocum *Polysyndeton* esto. 65
Membrum interjecto sermone *Parenthesis* auget. 66
Syllabicum adjectum sit vocis fine *Parolce*. 67

### In Defectu.

Dicitur *Elleipsis* si ad sensum dictio desit. 68
Unius verbi ad diversa reductio *Zeugma*. 69

### EXEMPLA.

62. Thymbre, *pro* Thymber. 63. Olli, *pro* illi; vol-g 65.
Fataque fortunasque virûm, moresque, manusque. 66.
Credo equidem (nec vana fides) genus esse Deorum. 67.
Numnam, *pro* num : adesdum, *pro* ades. 68. Non est solvendo, *supple* aptus; Dicunt, *supple*, illi. 69. Nec folium, nec arundo agitatur vento, (i. e. nec folium agitatur, nec arundo agitatur vento.)

### DERIVATIONES.

62. à μετά, trans, & τίθημι pono. 63. ab ἀντί, contra, & τίθημι, pono. 64. à πλεονάζω, redundo. 65. à πολύ, multum, & συνδέω, colligo. 66. à παρεντίθημι, interjicio. 67. à παρέλκω, protraho. 68. ab ἐλλείπω, prætermitto. 69. à ζευγνύμι, jungo.

*Metathesis* a letter's place doth change,    62
So that the word appear not new or strange.
*Antithesis* doth change the very letter;    63
A vowel for vowel as authors think it better.

### Figures of Excess in Syntax.

A *Pleonasmus* hath more words than needs,    64
And, to augment the emphasis, exceeds.
In *Polysyndeton* conjunctions flow,    65
And ev'ry word its cop'lative must show.
*Parenthesis* is independent sense,    66
Clos'd in a sentence () by this double fence.
*Parolce* particles to words apply,    67
Yet add no more to what they signify.

### Figures of Defect in Syntax.

*Elleipsis* drops a word to shorten speech,    68
And oft a sentence too t' omit doth teach.
*Zeugma* repeats the verb as often o'er    69
As construing words come after as before.

#### EXAMPLES.

62. Cruds *for* Curds.    63. Tye *for* tie; furnisht *for* furnished; exprest *for* expressed.    64. With my ears I heard it; I saw it with mine Eyes.    65. Fear and Joy and Hatred and Love seized the Mind by Turns.    66. I believe indeed (nor is my Faith vain) that he is the Offspring of the Gods.    67. He evermore *for* ever feeds. 68. True, *for* it is true.    69. Nor Leaf nor Reed is stirred by the Wind, (i. e. nor Leaf is stirred nor Reed is stirred by the Wind.)

#### TERMS ENGLISHED.

62. Transposition.    63. Opposition.    64. Superfluity. 65. Many Copulatives.    66. Interposition of Words.    67. Prolonging.    68. An Omission.    69. A Joining.

Personam, genus, et numerum conceptio triplex
Accipit indignum, *Syllepsis* sub magè digno. 70
*Dialyton*, tollit juncturam & *Asyndeton* æquè. 71


In CONTEXTU.

Est vocum inter se turbatus *Hyperbaton* ordo. 72
Quod meruit primum vult *Hysteron* esse secundum. 73
Casu transposito submutat *Hypallage* verba. 74
*Hellenismus* erit phrasis aut constructio Græca. 75
Voce interposità per *Tmesin* verbula scindas. 76
Jungit *Hyphen* voces, nectitque ligamine in unam. 77


EXEMPLA.

70. Ego, tu, & frater, (i. e. nos) legimus, &c. 71. Rex, miles, plebs, negat illud. 72. Vina, bonus quæ deinde cadis onerârat Acestes littore Trinacrio, dederatque abeuntibus, heros dividit. 73. Nutrit peperitque. 74. Necdum illis labra admovi, *pro* necdum illa labris admovi. 75. Desine clamorum. 76. Quæ mihi cunque placent, *pro* quæcunque mihi placent. 77. Semper-virentis Hymetti.


DERIVATIONES.

70. à συλλαμβάνω, comprehendo. 71. à διαλύω, dissolvo;—ab α, non, & συνδέω, connecto. 72. ab ὑπερβαίνω, transgredior. 73. ab ὕςερον, posterius. 74. ab ὑπὸ, sub, & ἀλλάττω, muto. 75. ab ἑλληνίζω, Græcè loquor. 76. à τέμνω, vel τμάω, seco, scindo. 77. ab ὑφ᾽, sub, & ἕν, unum.

## ART OF RHETORIC.

*Syllepsis*, in more worthy, comprehends    70
The less; and former's preference defends.
*Asyndeton*, or, (which the same implies,)    71
*Dialyton*, the cop'lative denies.

### In the CONTEXT.

*Hyperbaton* makes words and sense to run    72
In order that's disturb'd; such rather shun.
*Hysteron* doth misplace both words and sense,    73
And maketh last, what's first by just pretence.
*Hypallages* from case to case transpose;    74
A liberty that's never us'd in prose.
'Tis *Hellenismus* when we speak or write    75
In the like style and phrase the Greeks indite.
By *Tmesis* words divided oft are seen,    76
And others 'twixt the parts do intervene.
*Hyphen* does words to one another tie,    77
With such a dash as this (-) to know it by.

#### EXAMPLES.

70. I and my Brother, (i. e. we) go out to play. 71. Faith, Justice, Truth, Religion, Mercy dies. 72. Wealth, which the old Man had rak'd and scrap'd together, now the boy doth game and drink away; (*for* now the boy doth game and drink away Wealth, which the old Man had rak'd and scrap'd together.) 73. He was bred and born, *for* born and bred at London. 74. Cups, to which I never mov'd my Lips, *for* Cups which I never mov'd to my Lips. 75. I kept him from to die, (i. e. from Death.) 76. What crime soever, *for* whatsoever crime. 77. Purple-coloured.

#### TERMS ENGLISHED.

70. Comprehension. 71. Disjoined, or without a Copulative. 72. A passing over. 73. Placing after. 74. A Changing. 75. A Græcism, or Greek Phrase. 76. Dividing. 77. Uniting.

Personam, numerum, commutat *Enallage*, tempus 78
Cumque modo, genus et pariter. Sic sæpe videbis.
*Antimeria* solet vice partis ponere partem. 79
Digna præire solet postponere *Anastrophe* verba. 80
\*Tertia personæ alterius quandoque reperta est. 81
*Synthesis* est sensu, tantùm non congrua voce. 82
Et casu substantivat† *apponuntur* eodem. 83
*Antiptosis* amat pro casu ponere casum. 84

### PROSODIÆ.

M necat *Ecthlipsis;* sed vocalem *Synalæpha*. 85

### EXEMPLA.

78. Ni faciat, *pro* faceret, &c.  79. Sole recente, *pro* recenter orto.  80. Italiam contra, *pro* contra Italiam.  81. \**Evocatio*. Populus superamur ab illo: ego præceptor doceo.  82. Turba ruunt; pars maxima cæsi.  83. †*Appositio*. Mons Taurus, Urbs Athenæ.  84. Urbem, (*pro* urbs,) quam statuo, vestra est.  85. Si vit' inspicias, *pro* si vitam inspicias: Si vis anim' esse beatus, pro si vis animo esse beatus; viv' hodie, *pro* vive hodie.

### DERIVATIONES.

78. ab ἐναλλάττω, permuto.  79. ab ἀντί, pro, & μέρος, pars.  80. ab ἀναςρέφω, retrò verto.  81. ab evoco.  82. à συντίθημι, compono.  83. à προςτίθημι, appono.  84. ab ἀντί, pro, & πτῶσις, casus.  85. ab ἐκθλίβω, elido;—à συναλείφω, conglutino.

*Enallages* change person, number, tense, 78
Gender and mood, on any slight pretence.
By *Antimeria* for one part of speech 79
Another's put, which equal sense doth teach.
*Anastrophe* makes words that first should go 80
The last in place; verse oft will have it so.
By *Evocation* we the third recall 81
In first or second person's place to fall.
A *Synthesis* not words but sense respects; 82
For whose sake oft it strictest rules rejects.
By *Apposition* substantives agree 83
In case; yet numbers different may be.
By *Antiptosis* you may freely place 84
One, if as proper, for another case.

### Figures of Prosody.

*Ecthlipsis* M in th' end hath useless fix'd, 85
When vowel or H begins the word that's next.

#### EXAMPLES.

78. Alexander fights, *for* Alexander fought, &c. 79. He is new, *for* newly come Home. 80. He travell'd England through, *for* through England. 81. We the people are subject. 82. The Multitude rushes, *or* rush upon me. 83. Mount Taurus. The City Athens. 84. The City which I mean is yours, *for* the City is yours, which I mean. 85. *Peculiar to the Latins;* as, si vit' inspicias, *for* si vitam inspicias.

#### TERMS ENGLISHED.

78. A Change of Order. 79. One part for another. 80. Inventing. 81. Calling forth. 82. A Composition. 83. Nouns put in the same Case. 84. A Case put for a case. 85. A Striking out.

*Systole* ducta rapit : correpta *Diastole* ducit.     86
Syllaba de binis confecta *Synæresis* esto.     87
Dividit in binas partita *Diæresis* unam.     88

### EXEMPLA.

86. Stetĕrunt, *pro* stetērunt ; naufrāgia, *pro* naufrăgia.
87. Alveo—dissyllabum, *pro* Alveo—trissyllabo.    88. Evoluisset, *pro* Evolvisset.

### DERIVATIONES.

86. à συςέλλω, contraho ;—à διαςέλλω, produco.    87. à συνείρω, contraho.    88. à διαιρέω, divido.

### FINIS.

By *Synalœpha* final vowels give way,  85
That those in front of following words may stay.
A *Systole* long syllables make short:  86
The cramp'd and puzzled poet's last resort.
*Diastole* short syllables prolongs,  86
But this, to right the verse the accent wrongs.
*Synæresis*, whenever it indites,  87
Still into one, two syllables unites.
*Diæresis* one into two divides;  88
By which the smoother measure gently glides.

### EXAMPLES.

85. Si vis anim' esse beatus, *for* si vis animo esse beatus.  86. Stetĕrunt *for* stetērunt.  86. Naufrāgia *for* Naufrăgia.  87. Alveo, a dissyllable, *for* Alveo, a Trissyllable.  88. Evoluisset *for* Evolvisset.

### TERMS ENGLISHED.

85. A mingling together.  86. A Shortening.  86. Lengthening.  87. A Contraction.  88. A Division.

**THE END.**

CPSIA information can be obtained
at www.ICGtesting.com
Printed in the USA
BVHW061048140119
537774BV00028B/1719/P